Searching For The Light

Foreword

This book is written in an effort to help people find a healthier, happier and more productive way to live and meet their needs. All of the information in this book has been compiled, collected and interpreted throughout my adult life as a result of education, training, experience, and things I have learned from others. I want to thank everyone who has contributed to my knowledge and experience in life. This includes the many authors, scholars, educators, trainers, clients, and ordinary people who have shared their knowledge and experiences with me. I offer people solutions, skills, and knowledge too not only understand why life can be so problematic, but change they're thinking and ways they meet they're needs. This book will help people to learn to manage their relationships, families and communities in a manner that will build a support system and result in a healthy responsible and peaceful lifestyle. I am trying to develop this as my interpretation of a large eclectic body of knowledge that already exists in literature. I will make every effort to give people credit for the information in this book that I use. In the event that I don't give due credit I refer you to the internet, just use your search of choice, I.E. Google to look up the subject or person I am referring to or look on Wikipedia to find more information and insight into the field of discussion.

Ed Wagoner

Introduction

As we look at the population of our country we realize that many people are not as healthy personally as they could be. Many people have difficulties in their lives managing relationships, jobs, money, and their health. The divorce rate is over 50% and civil suits are soaring due in part to poor conflict resolution skills and an increasing lack of desire to work things out with people we have conflicts with. Many of these people are not happy with their lives and want to make changes but fall into the category of not wanting to seek help in learning new skills and developing tools to help them avoid problems in their everyday lives. Some people continue to cause others and themselves grief until they hopefully learn to make changes to avoid problems, usually through trial and error. This is why self-help books and videos are so popular because we are seeking information and knowledge on our own to improve our lives. Our rights and freedoms in this country give us the ability to make mistakes and solve our own problems as best we can so long as we do not cross the line of violating other people's rights. This is a good thing and I support it.

About the Author

Eddie L. Wagoner worked for twenty-three years in Children's Protective Services in Texas. He retired from The Texas Dept. Of Protective and Regulatory Services in 1999 and had a private counseling practice in Grayson and Fannin Counties in Texas until 2020 when he retired. In CPS Mr. Wagoner had the opportunity to participate in and conduct many training seminars dealing with families, children and the abuse and neglect of children. He worked regularly with both victims and perpetrators of abuse from a child protective, family social work and individual and family counseling perspective. Mr. Wagoner has attended training conducted by nationally recognized experts in the field of child development and children's needs and in the field of sexual abuse and sex offender treatment. Mr. Wagoner holds a Masters Degree in Psychology, was a Licensed Professional Counselor, a Licensed Clinical Social Worker, and a Licensed Sex Offender Treatment provider in Texas. He worked regularly with all area agencies to coordinate services to both children and adults in the community.

Mr. Wagoner has had extensive training and experience working in related fields such as drug and alcohol abuse, anger management, conflict resolution, relationship building, marital problems, life skills, parenting training, social and employment skills and education. This includes

Ed Wagoner

assessing the psychosocial and health needs and making community referrals for these clients. Mr. Wagoner is familiar with and worked regularly with all of the social services and support agencies in the community's he worked in and all governmental agencies providing services to client populations. Mr. Wagoner has taught Child Growth and Development and Psychology courses at Grayson Co. College and Collin County Community College. Mr. Wagoner has contracted with Community Supervision and Corrections, TDCJ, Federal Probation and Parole, in both Fannin and Grayson Co.'s to provide Sex Offender treatment and management on both a group and individual basis for the last 20 years. Mr. Wagoner has contracted with the Family Crisis Center and the Child Advocacy Center in Fannin Co. to provide victims services. Mr. Wagoner contracted with the Child Guidance Clinic of Texoma to present the Kids Hurt Program in Fannin County. In addition Mr. Wagoner provided expert witness testimony in sex-offender cases for the Fannin Co. District Attorney's office.

Mr. Wagoner has spent his career working with individuals and families who were experiencing troubles related to their functioning and choices which led to social and criminal problems. This experience along with his education and training has allowed him to develop insight into human behavior and problems. This has encouraged him to write this book hoping to provide knowledge and tools to persons with turmoil in their lives.

Searching For The Light

One of his goals was to offer individuals and their families, who have been convicted of criminal offenses and who have been or are currently incarcerated to find the knowledge and skills to change their thinking and behavior, to find the way to a peaceful and healthy life. Another goal is to help individuals and families who are having difficulties in their lives, who have not committed a criminal offence, to make the choices that will lead to healthier outcomes and relationships. To do no harm and strive to help others!

Ed Wagoner

Copyright@ 2024 by Ed Wagoner

All rights reserved. No part of this book may be used or reproduced in any manner whatsoever without written permission except in the case of information available on Wikipedia or in the bibliography.

First Edition: 2024

KDP ASIN BODKB69W28
ISBN-13   979-8-218-53746-3

I dedicate this book to my Family, Friends, and to all the people I have met in my Counseling Practice over the past 30 years, on both sides of the line. If I have brought any peace into your life in the past or bring peace to anyone in the Future then I accomplished my life's goal. I have found the Light!

Searching For The Light

Contents

Foreword..........1
Introduction 2
About the Author..........3
Chapter I Everyone can be a Good Person..........9
Chapter II Before We Were Born..........18
Chapter III Are People born good or bad..........22
Chapter IV Families..........32
Chapter V Overprotected..........36
Chapter VI Childhood..........40
Chapter VII Cooperation..........45
Chapter VIII The Eternal Internal Conflict..........54
Chapter IX Immediate Gratification..........59
Chapter X Steps for Change..........68
Chapter XI Anger Management..........88
Chapter XII Autonomy and Empathy..........101
Chapter XIII Self-Concept and Self-Esteem 106
Chapter XIV Needs and Relationships..........110
Chapter XV Sexual Behavior..........117
Chapter XVI Becoming a Wise Person..........124

Ed Wagoner

Chapter XVII Core Values and Basic Beliefs
....128
Chapter XVIII SPIRITUALITY....................148
BIBLIOGRAPHY 155

Chapter I

Everyone can be a Good Person

Everyone can be a good person. They most likely have done wrong things. Perhaps they have violated the rules of society, done hurtful things, even to themselves, or broken the law, but that does not make them a bad person. It only means that they have made bad choices, engaged in harmful behavior, developed some bad habits, and learned some unhealthy ways to meet their needs.

So to begin this journey it is very important that you know that every person is, inside, a good person, because all people are born with the capacity to be good. No one is born evil or harmful, (I will address this more in the next chapter) but anyone can develop patterns in life that create hurt and harm for themselves and for others.

Everyone is a good person, and though that goodness may be buried under a lot of questionable choices, what is good can be brought back to light and they can change for the better and feel good again.

Every person has the capacity to take responsibility for his or her life and become a caring individual. That is where we must begin, with becoming able to feel the needs and hurts of others as well as your own. It is called developing empathy.

No matter what a person may have done in the past, they have the ability to change and grow. Growing and changing may be slow, it may take time, but it can happen. If they work to learn and are willing, they can begin to make changes in their life and be able to feel and say again, "Yes, I am a good person."

Each person can learn to follow the rules and laws of society and not be in conflict with the world around them. They can learn to change so that they follow the basic rules of life that help keep their self, their family and society safe. This is accepting the "social contract". If they learn these rules and abide by them it will mean that there will be a lot less pain or conflict in their life.

Having less pain and difficulty in life is a wonderful goal. It can be achieved. First they have to begin to believe in their self and believe that they can change and grow. It will take work, sometimes very hard work.

Getting Started

We hear the statement that all people are born equal. This may be true in the eyes of God but when it comes to having social skills that allow people to live and function in a healthy and more trouble free way we all start out different. Each person has to learn the skills and develop the tools that allow them to co-exist with other humans to avoid unnecessary conflict and its consequences to themselves and to the people they care about.

    Some people start life with inherited or developmental deficits which create ongoing problems for them and people they deal with. Many of these deficits are obvious such a birth defects, genetic disorders, mental retardation, and mental illness. Others are not so easily seen and are characterized by the way the individual interacts or functions in social settings. For example, some people inherit the probability that they will develop mental problems like Schizophrenia, Bi-polar disorder and Attention Deficit Disorder. If they do develop these neurological disorders it affects their ability to learn, stay focused, and get along with other people they live with or form relationships with. This frequently leads to relationship, job, and legal problems. People who have serious mental disorders like schizophrenia are usually detected, diagnosed and treated relatively early with good results, if they have good support around them and are willing to take the psychotropic medications prescribed to them. People who develop Bi-polar disorder are harder to recognize and can go through life undiagnosed and untreated. These individuals are prone to have difficulty maintaining relationships, keeping jobs, and frequently turn to drugs and alcohol to self medicate. This can lead to more serious problems later on. Individuals with attention deficit disorder may have trouble focusing and staying on task at work or when they need to multitask. This also can lead to frustration and anger in school, their lives and relationships. It can lead to problems of self concept that may cause them to feel they are not as capable as other people. Some people are what we call "Sociopaths" This is a personality disorder that is difficult to change. I will talk more about them later.

Role Models

Most of us love our parents and do not want to hear anything negative about them. I need to say that I agree with this line of thought and am not placing responsibility on who a person becomes on anyone. We are looking at the factors that may have shaped choices like how they learned to meet their needs and solved their conflicts. First and foremost they have to accept responsibility for who they are and what they do. But it helps a lot to have insight into how they came to make those choices. Some of the things I say may not fit your experiences but can help you understand why people are unique individuals and at the same time have many of the same issues.

If a person is lucky they have had good parents or role models in their life that teach and guide them to be a fairly healthy individual. This often allows them to feel good about their self and have reasonably good social skills that let them function appropriately and stay out of trouble.
Unfortunately a lot of us have or had parents (or a

parent), or were raised by someone who, though well meaning, didn't have the skills or ability to be a good teacher or role model. They may have had problems themselves they just couldn't get beyond. Individuals who are conceived by immature, unaware or dysfunctional parents frequently develop behavioral problems either prenatally (from conception to birth) or in the early stages of childhood development. For example mothers who drink excessively, do drugs, smoke, live in an abusive or chaotic relationship deliver babies who are frequently pre-mature, with low birth weight, irritable and insecure with their environment. If the child continues to live with any of these problems their ability to learn healthy social skills is significantly impaired. These individuals start out life with problems and frequently develop coping behaviors that also create difficulties for them as they go through life. Children who grow up in these types of environments often have to take care of themselves. They learn to meet their needs and get what they want sometimes in ways that are harmful to others and self-destructive to themselves. For example, they learn to violate the rights of others and break the rules and laws of society to get what they want; this leads to problems in relationships and problems in their communities.

Ed Wagoner

Family Patterns

Growing up in families that are stable and with parents that love us is certainly an asset but does not necessarily mean that we are going to grow up secure and have a good self-concept. It also does not mean that we will have good social skills and that our lives will be trouble free. Unfortunately our society does not place a high value on training people to be parents or on teaching children to have good social skills that help them avoid social and legal problems. This leaves many well meaning parents practicing parenting that they learned from their parents through trial and error. All parents are human and subject to making mistakes and acting in emotional and sometimes irrational ways while raising children. Parents do what they believe is right but since they are frequently unaware of what may create problems for their children they sometimes practice a variety of inconsistent parenting techniques which develop problem behaviors and thinking in their children. For example, parents do not want to see their kids suffer or do without so they often do not follow through with consequences they have placed on their children. This teaches children that they can often get away with inappropriate behavior and that consequences are not enforced. Some parents discipline when they are angry or use anger and force to make their children do what they want them to do. This anger and force is frequently learned by children at an early age and used with peers and weaker individuals. Another pattern is that children may learn to be passive around someone they fear (an authority figure) and become deceptive and passive aggressive to get what they want. Learning to lie and secretly do things the parent does not approve of. Parents sometimes overindulge and protect their children from consequences that would help them adapt and learn better skills. These individuals often learn to become self-centered and to get what they want at others expense. These patterns of behavior are carried into adulthood and frequently practiced in relationships, in their work life, and are used to get around following the laws and rules of society. There are many other behaviors and skills we learn growing up that may help us get what we want or avoid punishment. Many of these skills hurt us when we reach adulthood and have to deal with people who expect and demand that we are responsible and follow the norms and laws of society.

    The theory is that many people bring into this world or learn behaviors and skills in childhood that are ingrained and become a part of their skills to cope and deal with life. Some of these people cannot see or do not understand how these learned behaviors and unhealthy coping skills affect their lives. As a result they do not have insight as to how their thinking and behavior contributes to the problems they have. This leads them to continue repeating behaviors that cost relationships, money, freedom, control over their lives, and peace of mind.

Ed Wagoner

The reality is that life is difficult and unfair for most people. We all have challenges we must overcome, and choices that can take us in either a positive or a negative direction in life. There are always going to be people who are more fortunate and appear to have a better deal than we do. We get frustrated with life when we feel we are trying as hard as we can to succeed and things just keep going wrong. There is nothing equal or fair about this, but it is a reality we all have to accept and learn to deal with.

The Importance of Change

People must understand the importance of change. You may have heard the quote "If you keep on doing what you've always done you will keep on getting what you always got." it's true. To be successful, people have to change the way they think in many aspects of life, they also have to change the way they meet their needs, solve problems and conflicts. They must learn new social skills that allow them to manage life in a healthy, responsible, and peaceful way.

This is a lot easier than you may think; most people learn some or all of these skills growing up as children in healthy, together families. Life is still difficult and full of opportunities to make bad choices so we all have to work hard at managing our lives. These skills and thinking processes are not difficult to learn or complicated to understand. They require only one thing; the desire to change your life and the commitment to internalize these skills, values, and thoughts into your life. This is not impossible, but sometimes difficult to do on your own. The belief is that 25% of all people will learn to overcome most of their problems on their own with little outside help. Another 25% will never overcome their problems because they won't make changes or they continue to blame others for all their misfortunes. (I.E. sociopaths) The remaining 50% can go either way. This may be the group that someone you know falls in and are the most likely to succeed given the information and skills they need to change. This book will help to understand how people learn to make choices and think in healthy and more positive ways. They can learn the information and skills they need. If they do they will be a healthier and happier person who now has the tools to change and take control of their life when they are ready to do so. This effort to change is a life's work. This means that none of us will ever be perfect and we can always learn new ways and skills to make our lives better.

Ed Wagoner

Chapter II

Before We Were Born

We each were born into a family and grew up in that family circle into the person we are now. Every family is different. Some families work better together than others, but all were trying to make it work. Like everything else there is good and bad in all families, positive and negative characteristics. If we are going to understand ourselves now, we need insight into the kind of family into which we were born and how we grew up there and how that family and its patterns shaped our early life. This is a complex subject with many different sides to it.

First is to understand that we were being shaped into the kind of person we are now before we were ever born. Our personalities were no doubt being formed even in our mother's womb.

Let's suppose that during pregnancy your mother became very fearful or angry. Imagine that she experienced great anxiety or some problem or trauma that upset her badly. It is possible that these feelings were communicated to you during that period. A child may be born with some of those emotions already inside—with a sense of fear toward the outside world, or greater irritability than the normal child.

Searching For The Light

Some children are exposed to chemicals in the womb such as drugs, caffeine, cigarette smoke or alcohol, and this affects their mental or emotional abilities. Children whose mother's abused alcohol may have physical problems' external or internal. Children whose mother's abused drugs often have emotional problems that may not surface until adolescence. In some cases it makes a child less able to fend for themselves in the world, or grow up in a normal way. They have either physical or mental deficiencies, or they are inclined to have emotional feelings like insecurity or anger before they can even think about whether the world is or is not a safe or secure place.

It is possible to see that these circumstances before birth and in early infancy can distort the very beginning of a person's life. The result may be that a child had an early sense of fear that their needs would not be met. In many children this results in that infant being more irritable, more demanding, more discontented expressed in crying and distress.

Let's assume that a mother or father was doing the best that they could do, but because they were young and inexperienced—they actually didn't know how to respond to all of the difficulties in life. Perhaps they were quite young themselves when their child was born, and, in fact, like any young person, they were trying as best they could not only to do right for the child, but to also meet their own needs.

Ed Wagoner

Life in this world is not easy. No one is perfect, and neither is any family. Some have more difficulty than others. Usually parents try to do the best they can—even if they are less than perfect. We should try and understand this effort, and respect it, though we can now see that in some ways it may have been difficult for everyone. We may have had issues because of that environment, but wherever we are now, we can make changes starting by understanding in a better way, the beginnings of our lives. That will give us insight in how to change now.

It is easier to build boys
than to mend men.
Unknown Author

The child is the Father to the Man
Unknown Author

What a father says to his children
is not heard by the world,
but it will be heard by posterity.
Jean Paul Richter

As a substitute father for hundreds of youths
over the past thirteen years,

Searching For The Light

I've yet to encounter a young person in trouble
whose difficulty could not be traced
to the lack of a strong father image in the home
Paul Anderson

My mother was the most beautiful woman I
ever saw.
All I am I owe to my mother.
George Washington

Ed Wagoner

Chapter III

Are People born good or bad

To some degree, we have resolved the question of whether people are born equal. Another challenging question to consider is whether people are born bad or born good. By good or bad I mean are we predisposed to be basically self centered, selfish and inconsiderate in nature and have to be socialized and taught to be responsible and considerate humans? Or are we basically good at birth and learn to be bad by growing up in an unhealthy and dysfunctional environment, or learn to make choices that serve our needs at the expense of others? To throw in another curve, there is another theory. B.F Skinner, a popular behaviorist believed people were born with a blank slate. In other words they could and were molded by their environment and personal experiences to become whoever they turned out to be.

I believe that the reality of whether we are born bad or good is complex and ties into the issue of equality we have already discussed. We all start out differently in life and we all start out a lot alike. Some of us have deficits we are challenged to overcome and some of us have assets we fail to use. A fundamental belief I hold is we all have the capacity to be good people and we must choose at some point in life to do good things or to do bad or hurtful things. I believe there are periods in our lives when we do not possess the skills or have the knowledge to know (or choose to ignore), the fact that behaviors we engage in are harmful to others and to ourselves. Childhood is one of those periods where we need guidance and direction to help us learn skills and thinking that allows us to function in a healthy responsible manner. If we do not get proper guidance and direction in childhood or we do not accept the guidance and values we are exposed to, and we do not develop good self-esteem and a strong value system then we will still grow into adults with learned skills and behaviors that may meet our needs to some degree but have consequences that follow afterwards. These skills usually involve immediate gratifiers which I will address more. If these skills and behaviors are not balanced with the expectations of others and society then we experience problems in one or more areas of our lives and practice behaviors that hurt others and ourselves.

As a person we must separate who we are from what we do. It is the behavior that is bad and not the person. We are all basically good people. We do problematic things in an effort to meet our needs and solve problems in our lives. We learn these unhealthy skills along with good skills and values as we grow up. Things like being deceptive and manipulative to get what we want and stay out of trouble. We may learn to be aggressive to get what we want rather than learning good social skills like patience, cooperation and consideration for others feelings and needs. We all have made mistakes and done things that hurt others. We must learn from

Ed Wagoner

these mistakes and become responsible, fair, and considerate in our thinking and behavior and this is what makes our behavior good instead of bad. So to begin this process it is very important that you know that every person is a good person, because all people are born with the capacity to be "good." No one is born evil or harmful, with a few exceptions, but anyone can develop patterns in life that create hurt and harm for themselves and for others. No matter what you may have done in the past, you have the ability to change and grow.

Each person can learn to follow the rules and laws of society and not be in constant conflict with the world around them. That is true of you as well. It is called accepting the social contract. You learn to change so that you follow the basic rules and behaviors that help keep society safe around you. If you learn these rules and abide by them it will mean that there will be a lot less pain or conflict in your own life. Having less pain and difficulty in your life is a wonderful goal. It can be achieved, but you have to begin by believing in yourself. Believe that you can change and grow, and that it will take work, sometimes hard work.

Every person has the capacity to take responsibility for his or her life right now and become a caring individual. That is where we must begin, by developing the ability to feel the needs and hurts of others as well as yourself; we must start by making the commitment that it does not happen anymore. Growing and changing may be slow, it may take time, but it can happen. If you work hard to learn and are willing, you can begin to make changes in your life and be able to feel and say again, "Yes, I am a good person."

Somewhere In-Between

It is important that we understand that we are all different and we are not at one extreme or the other when it comes to being bad or good on the above scale. Most of us fall somewhere in-between with both good qualities and skills, but also with some skills and inadequate tools to help us deal with life's challenges. The reality of life is most of us go into adulthood practicing both good and bad behaviors and thinking in our lives. This makes us human. What separates us is that some people want to do well but may not have the necessary skills and knowledge to change. Others are satisfied to stay the way they are, holding on to the beliefs and thinking errors that say they are okay just the way they are and all of their problems are someone else's fault.

In psychology if we apply the normal bell curve to many types of human behavior it can somewhat accurately predict human behavior. We will predict that on one extreme 25% of all people will learn to correct their own behaviors and problems in life by learning from their mistakes and from those of others, without outside help or intervention. On the other extreme another 25% of all people who have difficulty in life will not change and will not learn

Ed Wagoner

from the problems they experience in life and are destined to keep repeating a cycle of problem behavior and thinking that insures ongoing difficulties and instability in life. The majority of people (or the middle 50%) can go either way. These are the people who benefit the most from changing their thinking and behavior by learning new skills and techniques to meet their needs and solve conflicts in life. Aside from the theory of the bell curve in practice, I believe a much smaller percentage of people fall into the "I can't be or don't want to be helped" category. There is a small group of people in life that can be characterized as anti-social or sociopathic. These individuals truly are incapable of feeling empathy and are incapable of finding fault in themselves. They are regularly involved in conflict with social and/ or criminal problems and their lives are chaotic as a whole. Yet these individuals believe all of their difficulties are someone else's fault. These are the people who never do anything wrong and will never say I'm sorry. These are extremely difficult people to help and change. If you are or have been in a relationship with a person like this, they will make your life miserable.

Aside from sociopaths the vast majority of people understand they play a role in the problems they have and want to improve their lives. They are capable of growing and changing once they overcome their own inner resistance. But herein lays the big challenge. The reality is the majority of people are reluctant to seek help or take the necessary steps to learn the skills, gather the knowledge, to make the changes critical to a better life. These people are by nature resistant to change. They find security in doing what they have learned and know and have not made the relationship between what they are doing and the outcome of their choices.

Growing Up Human

Growing up in the world is never easy, and neither is the world a safe place to be. We each make our own way the best we can. We learn and develop from what we experience and what is offered to us. Sometimes what we experience and what we learn turns out not to be the best for us after all. The family around us may not always know what to do, though probably they were trying to do the best they could. So we grow up with some things that are helpful and some things that are not. That is true for everyone.

When we're young, we didn't think about how our experiences affected us, but we tried to make sense out of the world anyhow, and respond to it in a way that would make us feel good and get our needs met. Let's also suppose that there were lacks or gaps in what was available to us, and that some of our needs don't get met, especially in the right way. Maybe we didn't feel fully loved or accepted for who we were. Perhaps we felt left out, or that something was missing, we were not as important as we wanted to feel.

Ed Wagoner

What humans try to do in those circumstances is to make up for those gaps. We try to feel wanted, or important the best way we can. We want to enjoy life and perhaps the easiest way to do it is by doing things that will make us feel better, but perhaps in violation of our rules or at the expense of other people. It may be that we learned that we could do things that made us feel better but we knew were not the right thing to do and get by with it. Nobody seemed to notice, and it got us what we wanted. Or we were deceptive in other ways that made it seem that we were enjoying life but in the end we actually were learning some bad habits.

At first these did not seem very important to us. If we got caught, we didn't suffer much because of it. So perhaps, then, we tried other things, more risky, and pushing the line of what was acceptable. If we got what we wanted, and again, we were not caught, then we might have been tempted to escalate the behavior, and our bad habits grew. You can see where this going and how it might, step-by-step affect our future.

Eventually, something was bound to happen that got us in trouble, perhaps bad trouble with the people around us, our community, or the law, and then things began to spiral downward. The ways we were meeting our immediate needs became a danger to us and to others, and because we had not learned other, better ways, we suddenly felt stuck.

Searching For The Light

Now this scenario is just one of many ways that people "grow up human" in an imperfect world. Some people seem to handle the difficulties of life better than others. We never know how it is going to turn out for each individual. We each have strengths and weaknesses. The people that seem to get in trouble the most have inner strengths, and the people that seem to avoid trouble also have weaknesses. Every individual is different and there are always good things to build on, and weaknesses to avoid. So anyone can learn new skills. And sometimes life provides us with "free lessons" along the way, and even from the difficult ones we can benefit from what happens to us. It all depends, of course, on how we use those lessons. No one need be stuck in only one pattern of life. We can all grow further as human beings.

Experience is a wonderful thing.
It enables you to recognize a mistake when you make it again.
Unknown Author

Nothing can bring you peace but yourself.
Ralph Waldo Emerson

Experience is not what happens to you,
it is what you do with what happens to you.

Ed Wagoner

Unknown Author

Experience is a hard teacher
because she gives the test first,
the lesson comes afterwards.
Vernon Law

Wisdom is born of mistakes;
confront error and learn.
J. Jelinek

Chapter IV

Families

Every person on earth has some type of a family relationship. Even if we were orphaned early in life, we still have a family of origin that gave us birth, and a family who helped raise us as children. Not all families are, of course, equal. Some are large and some are small. Some are easy to get along with, and some are difficult and troublesome, but we all have them and they play a major role in how we grow up.

A family is our first "school room." Our parents, brothers and sisters, grandparents, aunts and uncles were our first teachers. They may have had no education, or have been well educated, but they taught us nevertheless. The question is, of course, what lessons did we learn from these first teachers and their teachings?

Some parents are natural born teachers. Without formal education, they seem to know what a child needs. Other parents feel confused and frustrated by having children, maybe too early, or because they did not have "natural born" teachers in their early lives. Regardless of how we were taught, we learned many things just by watching the interactions around us, and internalize or reject the things that were said either directly to us or to others in our home.

Ed Wagoner

Now the fact is, not everything we learned or were taught helped us. Some things did, but some things may have put us at an early disadvantage. Suppose, for example, our family life was fairly strict, even abusive. Maybe our parents did not know how to raise children with fairness or a good understanding. They may have even taken out some of their frustrations on us when we young and did not fully understand how they affected us. We just knew that we felt bad, and we reacted in different ways—by withdrawing, or its opposite, by fighting back ourselves.

These early patterns have certainly left their mark upon us, and if we were wounded in some way, and did not know how to fully protect ourselves (and most children don't), we may have developed ways of surviving that later turned out to be harmful. For example, if our parents for whatever reason were too strict and even harmful in the way they raised us, to defend ourselves we may have become secretive, hiding from danger, or giving up on ourselves, feeling bad and thinking everything must be our fault. Or we may learned to be aggressive trying to get our needs met or to defend ourselves from criticism.

Every child is different, of course, and responds to his or her environment in unique own way. Many children that do grow up in what we might call "dysfunctional environments" remain healthy and become socially responsible people in later life. This fact has a lot to do with how a child adapts to the family of origin, and who he or she chooses as a model to act out patterns of behavior, and the skills and values which the child uses to form his or her identity. Other children learn to meet their needs in unhealthy and socially undesirable ways. They may learn to be deceptive in order to get what they want while avoiding consequences. Finally, some children may make friends with other children that have similar experiences, behavior and thinking patterns. The behavior of their group of friends reinforces these patterns and strengthens the undesirable ways in which that child begins to interact with society. But we can learn to act differently, even later in life and change the early patterns of behavior into something good.

Happy families are all alike;
Every unhappy one is unhappy in its own way.
Leo Tolstoy

The presidency is temporary,
but the family is permanent.
Yvonne de Gaulle

A real family man is one who looks at his new
baby as an addition
rather than a deduction.

Ed Wagoner

It is easier to build boys
than to mend men
A Danish Proverb

The chances are that you'll never be elected
President of the country,
Write the great American novel, or make a
million dollars,
stop pollution and racial conflict, or save the
world.
However valid it may be to work at any of
these goals,
There is another one of higher priority—to be
an effective parent.
Landrum R. Bolling

Chapter V

Overprotected

Not all families are created equal. In fact, they are all different. But there are patterns that you can see. As children, they begin learning patterns of good and bad behavior very early in life.

There is an interesting pattern of family life that often contributes to children learning unhealthy and dysfunctional ways to meet needs. We might not suspect that this kind of family would produce children that have problems in later life, but it does. Difficulties begin to occur when well-meaning parents over indulge, or spoil, their children. This is the opposite of neglect, abuse, or abandonment that is often perceived as the more important factors in later behavioral problems.

For infants it is critical that they have all of their physical and emotional needs met in a timely manner. This kind of care provides the sense of security and self-esteem which is the foundation of a healthy life. It allows the child to interact and explore its world with trust and confidence that its needs are going to be met. Childhood is a critical time, a window of opportunity, for children to learn the values they will need to become healthy adults.

The part of a child's nature that craves pleasure makes it to want more of all the good things it is experiencing. As he or she passes through this stage of development, it is normal in a child's nature to focus almost entirely on its own needs. At this stage, some children become demanding in wanting more and more, throwing a fit if his or her demands are not met. A parent may feel obliged to give in to this sort of behavior over and over again without setting any limits or the child suffering any consequences, believing that he or she is doing the right and loving thing.

That parent may also continue to indulge and defend the child against all critics of these growing demands or tantrum-like behavior. The result is, however, that the child grows up more and more self-centered, feeling that his or her needs are more important than anyone else's. The outcome is that this over-indulged child develops a sense of exaggerated self-importance early on that is linked to a lack of empathy for others. As this person interacts with the world and other people their behavior is not well tolerated and they may find themselves regularly having conflicts and problems, which they tend to see as the other person's fault. They have not learned to examine their role in contributing to these problems and see the other person or organization as the problem causer. This tends to allow them to see their world as unfair and critical and makes them angry at this unjust treatment. This sense of unfairness or unjustness allows the individual to justify taking advantage of opportunities that come available, or to consciously engage in behavior that brings them some advantage over others. This is one of the theories for the justification of antisocial and criminal behavior. That and the fact that most people who engage in criminal behavior don't think seriously about the consequences of being caught. (Robert Hare) This can also occur if the person chooses a group or sub-culture to identify with or as a role model that tolerates this type of thinking or behavior. The standards and rules tolerated by the group or sub-culture may become the acceptable rule for the individual and all who criticize will be seen as unfair or out to get the group as a whole.

As the child grows, his or her exaggerated sense of self importance is seen more and more in various forms of selfish thinking. Because the child has never really had to face the consequence for inappropriate behavior, believing that whatever problems occur in his or her life is always someone else's fault, so why take responsibility for any problems. As time goes on as a child grows up into his or her teenage years, we will likely see an individual who will be prone to have social problems, difficulties relating to other people and the norms of society, and become someone who is likely to take advantage of weaker people. Should this behavior continue into adulthood social problems may follow? As we can see, there is a direct link between over-indulgence and later difficulties.

Ed Wagoner

Some families can trace their ancestry back
three hundred years,
but can't tell you where the children were last
night.
Unknown Author

Some family trees suffer from lack of pruning.
Unknown Author

There are too many fathers who tie up their
hound dogs at night
and let their boys run loose.
Unknown Author

Could I turn back the time machine,
I would double the attention I gave my children
and go to fewer meetings.
J. D. Eppinga

Criticism from a friend
is better than flattery from an enemy.
Unknown Author

Chapter VI

Childhood

We each have a personality, that is, the unique way we present our inner selves to the outside world around us. That unique personality makes us special, who we are, the pattern of that personality we began in childhood. We can understand that the form of the pattern was set long before we even comprehended it. We can learn something about both its promises and its problems.

Personality types are actually strategies we began to learn in childhood to deal with our imperfect world. Before we ever realized what was happening, or what it meant, we began to develop certain responses as children to the world in which we grew up. Piaget called this an accumulation of errors which we balance with reality as we mature cognitively. These patterns of behavior were the best we could do as a child, and considering they were thought-up with the mind of the child, they were not that bad. Developmental psychologist (Piaget) help us understand a child's mind has to grow and develop to reason and process reality. This doesn't happen until we reach adolescence or longer. There is a significant difference in children in when they achieve this milestone. Children learn best from their peers, but what they learn is not always reality.

Ed Wagoner

Say, for example, we were trying to be ourselves in a world that did not always recognize, welcome, or support us, so we developed strategies to defend ourselves against what we felt was a lack of attention or support. To help us face this, we may have become too aggressive or too passive in trying to find a way to get our basic needs met. We may have felt we had to be deceitful or dishonest to get what we really wanted, attention from others. But in each of these cases, we were trying to fulfill our most fundamental needs the best way we could under the circumstances in which we found ourselves. Knowing this and beginning to understand what we were doing as children allows us to have more compassion for ourselves in those conditions. We can honor the child that tried so hard, but could not make everything come out exactly as we wanted it.

Or suppose, as another example, we felt supported and loved by our early environment: our parents, our brothers and sisters, our family. That world of our early childhood formed a "protective bubble" around us and helped us grow. We began to respond to the way our world saw us, the way it wanted us to be. Perhaps our order of birth gave us certain advantages, or we were encouraged to grow in a certain way which strengthened how we reacted and responded to the world. That encouragement from outside ourselves became a source of inner strength that we still carry around inside of us. We can begin to see and understand that now. We can work with it to strengthen the positive aspects of our personality and weaken the negative.

We can also understand what may have happened later as a result of both the problems and promises of our early up-bringing. If certain aspects of these patterns became larger and more fixed, perhaps we did not have any other better ways of dealing with the increasing complexity of the world that we began to experience. We may have become stuck in the old familiar patterns that we were used to, but these were too limited to really help us. Or we may have emphasized one aspect of our personality, the part that people responded to with positive feedback, and maybe other aspects were neglected. By seeing things in this way we can now have a better perspective on the way our lives unfolded. We can see some of the difficulties in which we now find ourselves more clearly, and we can actually begin to change things for the better. We can also draw upon the strengths we have and balance out where we may need some extra understanding and support.

Here are some positive aspects of personality that we may want to learn and include as a part of our inner resources, or to balance out things in our personality that we see as difficulties. For example, if we see that we used deception or dishonesty that made us feel guilty, then we can develop aspects such as honesty, transparency, genuineness and authenticity.

Ed Wagoner

If we often have what is called ego centered thinking and as a result are not fully aware of the needs of others. We focused on our own needs; we can begin to develop a sense of awareness of others, become more responsive when we see others in need.

For example if we treat events, people and even opportunities as a threat, and therefore cannot relax and feel at ease, then we can begin to learn to let go and be more at ease, more open and more spontaneous with life and not feel insecure or threatened or have to over-manage and be in control of everything. We have to learn to like ourselves and understand our past behavior does not have to define who we are as a person. We can change those behaviors and change who we are to everyone that matters.

We may have learned early to distrust the world, others, even ourselves, and we see relationships as a challenge, we can begin to gain a level of trust, faith in ourselves, and believe that there is something larger than ourselves that will make our life healthier. It is here now within our grasp.

The measure of a man is not determined by his show of outward strength, or the volume of his voice, or the thunder of his action. It is to be seen rather in terms of the strength of his inner self, in terms of the nature and depth of his commitments,

the sincerity of his purpose, and his willingness to continue "growing up."
Grade E. Poulard

Five or six-year old children can be taught to have optimistic attitudes. Parents can talk about past positive experiences. They can help their children to develop a sense of control, and display optimistic attitudes themselves.
Julius and Zelda Segal
"Raising an Optimist"

When you look at the world in a narrow way,
How narrow it seems!
When you look at it in a mean way,
How mean it is!
When you look at it selfishly,
How selfish it is!
But when you look at it in a broad, generous, friendly spirit,
what wonderful people you find in it!"
Horace Rutledge

Our destiny is not pre-determined for us;
We determine it for ourselves
Arnold Toynbee

Ed Wagoner

Chapter VII

Cooperation

Human beings are born into families which is a basic unit where individuals live together in mutual interdependence and cooperation. No family is perfect, of course, but the ideal is that the members of each family learn to live in some kind of harmony and balance where they can help meet the needs of every individual in the family group. That is the idea, and in normal families it seems to work fairly well. As we grow from infancy into childhood our social world expands out of the immediate family into an extended family of grandparents, aunts and uncles, cousins and family friends. Then we also begin to build a world around us that includes our own special friends, school-mates, but also other adults such as teachers and neighbors that become part of our world. In each case, like the immediate family we grew up in, in order to survive, we had to learn to cooperate with and work within that larger world with the skills we were learning of cooperation and understanding.

Understanding, empathy and cooperation with others are absolute necessary or we will not survive in the world. We cannot survive by simply fighting against the world around us, to live well. We must also learn how to really work with others. The question is, then how do we balance what seems to be opposites forces inside us that sometimes compete with one another. No doubt you have felt this struggle inside of you as you have experienced your life.

We are all aware that the affects of extreme anger and rage breaks the bonds of friendship and communication people. It can disrupt our lives and all the patterns of communication and cooperation we need to have in order to really live well in the world, but we feel anger boil up inside of us nonetheless. So what are we to do? How can we think about these competing forces?

Let's imagine that we are going to have to learn to manage the emotions of anger, just the way we do with other emotions like extreme sadness or joy. We are also going to need to learn to how to cooperate with the people around us. This will undoubtedly mean that we must learn new skills and let go of our angry behavior, or at least, learn what we can do it manage it better. This is called "anger management training."

In order to take the first step of working better with the people around us, we need to know that without cooperation we cannot really live well or get our needs met. So learning cooperation involves both giving and receiving. Often we have to give (even without thinking about getting anything in return) before we can start receiving. If we are open and generous with others, they in turn will tend to be open and generous with us. Of course, life is not perfect, and sometimes very unfair, but in general, people respond well to us when we act in a generous and open way toward them. So what we need is to observe our own behavior.

How often are we thinking only about ourselves, or at least, about ourselves first? How often do we pay any attention to others and how they are feeling? We could take a first good step by simply asking sincerely how someone else is, and what they are feeling. The next step, perhaps, is to act in a friendly and cooperative way. This may be with our words and the way we express ourselves, but more importantly it may be that we do some act of kindness and try to help someone with their immediate needs, perhaps even unexpectedly, when we're not really planning it. The third way is to do some planning in our own minds to see how we can help those we love and care about so that they know we are thinking about them and their needs. Doing this gets us away from always thinking and focusing on ourselves. Actually this can make us feel very good, and it is a way of creating a world around us that is cooperative and friendly, instead of unfriendly and hostile. These are first steps, but they are important ones.

Empathy and Cooperation With Others

Some animals are independent from birth, fish, turtles, reptiles of various kinds, for example. But the higher, more complex forms of life are dependent upon their mothers and fathers to provide and take care of them. Humans are like that. We are born needing the help of others or we will not survive. We grow up in families and societies that care for us. As a result we form bonds with the people around us that we love and who love us. You could say, then, that we are social creatures. Throughout our lifetime, we need one another. This need may lessen, of course, as we become older and more independent, but the truth is we will always need to make friends with and interact with other people because we need others to live. It is through others that we find jobs and make a living. Other people farm and provide food for us and our families. Other build and we have shelter. This is what it means to be human, to love and be loved by others.

Learning to cooperate with others, therefore, is something we begin doing with our mothers at a very early age. It was the way we learn to survive in the world. We are not born with instincts in the way many animals are, we have to learn and develop survival skills by watching, listening to, and learning from those around us. This requires that we learn to cooperate with others who have the same needs as we do.

Although we have the same or similar needs as everyone else, what we experience is that we do not always get our needs met when we want. Life is a give and take situation. We learn both to receive and to give help to others. Right from the

Ed Wagoner

beginning we have to learn to cooperate so we can better meet our own needs and wants. Sharing with others, therefore, is crucial, but some folk simply do not learn to share well. They want what they want when they want it, and everyone else "be damned" is often their attitude. This attitude ends up damaging the world, and even lessening the possibility that they will get what they need. People tend to resist a person like this. On the other hand, a person who is more cooperative usually ends up getting his or her needs met faster and with less resistance.

"It is easy to become so focused on myself and my needs that I have not noticed the needs of others. I haven't learned really to cooperate with others. So how do I do this? How do I learn empathy and sympathy for others? How do I learn to cooperate?"

We learn first by observation and listening both to our own needs but also finding out about others' needs. We might begin by observing and asking. It is important that we expand beyond our own thoughts and learn to hear what others think and feel. This is the first step in cooperation. We may not always agree with the opinions and thoughts of others, but we, at least, need to listen and learn how others feel and think. We need to also to express our own needs in a direct but non-threatening way. This is a second step in cooperation.

Searching For The Light

If we can do just these two, then we can learn not to be as self-centered and aggressive about always getting our way first. Cooperation means that sometimes we are first, but at other times we go last, and let others be first. It means that we learn not to use force, aggression, or to hurt others to get our way. But by listening and asking we learn to feel what others feel and have some sympathy and understanding for the way they feel.

Unknown Authors unless Named

You've got to have the blocking,
or you can't gain the yards.
Joe Perry

A lot of people are lonely because they build walls instead of bridges.

If you don't believe in cooperation,
look what happens when a car loses one of its wheels.

You cannot sink someone else's end of the boat
and still keep your own afloat.
Charles Bower

Ed Wagoner

A bundle of sticks is always stronger
than a single twig.

A little boy was playing all alone in the front
yard when a neighbor came along and asked
where his brother was, "Oh," he said, "he's in the
house playing a game of checkers.
I finished first."

Unknown Authors for the Below Sayings
Unless named

If you mind can conceive it,
and your heart can believe it,
then you can achieve it.

Hatred and anger are powerless when met with
kindness.

Kindness is the oil that takes the friction out of
life.

Searching For The Light

Be kind to unkind people—they need it the most.

Kindness pays most when you do not do it for pay.

"What shall I do to love my neighbor?"
"Stop hating yourself."
The student pondered those words for awhile
and then came back to say,
"But I love myself too much,
for I am selfish and self-centered.
How do I get rid of that?"

"Be friendly to yourself and your self
will be contented and it will set you free
to love your neighbor."

No person has ever been honored for what they have received;
always, for what they have given.

Give to the world the best you have,
and the best will come back to you.
Ella Wheeler Wilcox

Ed Wagoner

> Every time we hold our tongue instead of
> returning the sharp retort,
> show patience for another's faults,
> show a little more love and kindness;
> we are helping to stockpile more of these
> peace-bringing qualities
> in the world.
> *Constance Foster*

Chapter VIII

The Eternal Internal Conflict

The previous chapters have given you some insight into the many factors that influence your choices and behavior. I now want to help you gain a new understanding of a very great challenge that everyone has to deal with many times in their lives. There are two important forces at work within each of us which are known by various names. The ones we know best, perhaps, are the words good and evil. We each struggle with the forces of good and evil almost every day of our lives. And we see and experience it in the world around us as well.

Some people call these same forces by other names such as "the devil," and "the angel." These, they believe, sit on our shoulders and make suggestions to us. A famous neurologist and the Founding Father of Psychoanalysis in the early 20th century, Sigmund Freud, called these forces "the id" and the "superego" and suggested that every one of us had to deal with the struggle between these two parts of our being as a part of the way we develop an ego and a personality. Today we might call these forces by such terms as "immediate gratification" and "delayed gratification". The reason this is called delayed is because we almost always have to work for and towards the "good things" we want in life. It takes time to do that, and so we don't instantly get what

Ed Wagoner

we want. It is thus "delayed" until it is time to receive it.

    Inside of you is a "decision maker," known as the ego, who will decide which one of these influences will guide your behavior. The face-off between these two forces is an ongoing struggle within you and the battle often wages back and forth until we firmly decide just who we are and what values and guidelines we are going to accept and follow in our lives. Once again, we could see this as the conflict between the pursuit of instant pleasure (or immediate gratification) and our learned internal and external values over the long haul (delayed gratification). The outcome of this struggle to choose right from wrong has a powerful influence on the way we see ourselves and ultimately how we see our world. Equally important, the end result of this struggle also determines how the world will see us.

    The battle between good and evil does not have to end in our defeat, nor even in a stalemate. It can be an ongoing victory or success in life. But as any soldier in a battle knows, it takes vigilance and discipline to move forward across the battlefield of life. As we move forward in that battle one of the things we will encounter is that our basic desires for pleasure are often fueled by a manipulative society which leads us to believe that we must have certain things immediately in order to be happy or feel fulfilled. This idea is in all the media advertisements for clothes, cars, material possessions and even physical appearance, status and recognition. If we accept this part of our social structure, then in our desire for approval it is easy for a thinking error to occur that suggests we must get these things in any way we can, no matter what. We must have these things in to feel good about ourselves, equal to our peers and role models.

If allowed to run out of control, however, the pursuit of immediate pleasure can quickly move us to selfishly benefit ourselves at the expense of others. If we do not understand the power of its influence we will begin to experience thinking errors and use defense mechanisms to justify our wants and our behaviors. On the one hand, thinking errors and defense mechanisms gives us the excuse to pursue our desires in an unhealthy manner. But, on the other, if we understand the positive nature of this force we can channel its energy in a positive direction that will give us the drive we need to do good things with our lives and feel good about ourselves as person.

The force that pushes us to immediate gratification or pleasure, however, should never be discounted or thrown away. Instead, it should be seen as a necessary force within us since it provides us with the energy and drive we need to meet our goals and find a sense of enjoyment in life. If it is properly used it becomes a positive force that allows us to accomplish what we desire, and gives us the will and energy to accomplish

Ed Wagoner

good things that not only benefit ourselves, but those around us.

We each need to find pleasure in our lives in legal and socially responsible ways that do not cause harm to ourselves or anyone else. When we find pleasure in our life in ways that are socially acceptable as well as legal, we learn to enjoy life and feel good about ourselves and what is occurring around us. Things begin to move in a positive direction, and as we build one step upon another, things start to change for the better. This does not mean that there are no bumps in the road, or that we will not be tempted, or even at times fall back into unhealthy forms of behavior, but we realize that we always have another option to meet our needs.

>You find what you look for:
>Good or evil, problems or solutions.
>*John M. Templeton*

>The people who get on in this world are those who get up and look for circumstances they want and, if they can't find them, the make them.
>*--George Bernard Shaw*

>The way to mend the bad world is to create the right world.

Searching For The Light

--Ralph Waldo Emerson

You gotta accentuate the positive; eliminate the negative.
Latch on to the affirmative; don't mess with Mr. In-Between!
--Johnny Mercer singer in the 1940s

Ed Wagoner

Chapter IX

Immediate Gratification

Most people grow up in a fairly normal family. "Normal," meaning, not abused and not over-indulged. We may be exposed to reasonably good values by our parents, family and teachers. We may have been taught or exposed to the importance of things like honesty, kindness, and caring for our family, friends and neighbors. We know the difference between right and wrong. Unfortunately there are normal human thinking and behaviors that we are tempted to engage in almost every day, and these are not always in our best interest. We might call these "immediate gratifiers." We are enticed to do what brings us pleasure, to meet our immediate needs, or to do what gives us advantage at the expense of other persons or by violating some rule, guideline, or law of society.

We learn this pattern of behavior and accept it, thinking that it is necessary to find pleasure and happiness in life. Pleasure we can have now, or any time we want through immediate gratification. The famous psychologist, Sigmund Freud wrote that there is a part of every person's mind that pushes him or her to have pleasure. It is built right into us. Freud addressed this in his concept of human psyche, the Id, ego, and superego. Every person, therefore, must struggle with these impulses and drives for immediate pleasure. Most of us, with the exception people categorized as sociopaths, also have a higher knowledge of what is right and wrong. By using the basic values and morals we have been taught and are consciously aware of. We all have an understanding of right and wrong we just don't always apply it to our decision making at the time.

We start on a course of benefiting ourselves by being egocentric, frequently by making choices that benefit ourselves at the deception or harm to others. This may start simply by doing something our parents do not want us to do, but because we desire this thing or behavior we must act in a deceptive way by lying to cover our choices. We might start by sneaking out of the house, going places we know we are not supposed to go, or by smoking, drinking, doing drugs, and experimenting with sex. We may cheat on our homework, or take something that did not belong to us. We say to ourselves, "No big deal. No one will ever know." And often they don't. This goal we have achieved now serves as a rewarding experience and increases the probability we will do it again. If we get caught and there are proper and effective consequences then our probability to make this choice again is diminished. So if we are growing up in a less structured or less supervised environment we tend to learn and practice more deceptive behaviors because we are rewarding our desire for personal gain, pleasure and fun. This behavior is affected by our development of values and morals as we mature. These are also learned processes and affected by our environment and the

Ed Wagoner

influences and needs in our life. Let me say here that it is a normal part of exploring our identity to push the boundaries of our perceived limits. Ideally we learn this life skill and accept the social contract. The social contract is internalizing the social, civil, and legal rules of our country, our State, and our community. We make a personal commitment; internalize the value, to always do the right thing. It becomes a part of our thinking and choices so we don't let our subconscious desire for unhealthy pleasure play a role in our decision making. Now remember, nobody's perfect so this is something we have to continue to work on in our lives.

For most people this is a kind of experimentation in testing the limits and the rules and seeing what we can get away with. It can become an indulgence of our need for pleasure and a practice in getting things quickly and easily, and therefore becomes an "immediate gratifier." The need and desire for pleasure, fun, excitement, and happiness exists in all people. It is part of our challenge in life, however, to meet these basic needs in a legal and socially responsible way, accepting the social contract to do no harm to others. Ironically the legal and socially responsible way usually requires more work and more effort and time to achieve than what we may want to expend. It may also require resources like money, transportation and guidance from others. If these are not readily available to us, we may become frustrated and angry because some people seem to have the things we want, or feel we need, and we don't.

When we are in a state of frustration with unmet needs, it is easier and more probable that we will overlook the basic values and morals we have learned and convince ourselves that it is okay to have what we want, and alright to get it in a manner that is immediately available to us. We can call this way of reasoning, a "thinking error." A thinking error (or also clinically a "cognitive distortion") allows us to have what we want or do what we want to do without thinking about or repressing the potential consequences to ourselves and others, for example, that it's okay to do drugs, alcohol and sex in some combination because "I deserve" to be happy and need to feel good. Also, it is okay to steal, lie or manipulate if necessary to get what I want.

When our felt needs and desire are not being met, these drives and impulses can become almost overwhelming—powerful forces that affect our ability to make good choices. If we are presented with an opportunity to meet our immediate needs and have pleasure now, when we most want it, it becomes extremely difficult for us to say no. Also, if we are being encouraged or influenced by others to do these things, it becomes even more difficult to resist.

When we give in to immediate gratification or pleasure we often feel guilty and may tell ourselves we have done the wrong thing, made a wrong choice. But our minds also have a way of dealing with the guilt. In time we can put it all away and hide it in our unconscious. This is called, "repressing it." This is a basic defense mechanism that is a genetic part of our psyche. We subconsciously employ this to keep from feeling bad about the things we think and do on an ongoing basis. This is utilized by all people to some extent. We do this in order to keep from feeling bad about ourselves. A part of ego protection. We also use thinking errors to help us rationalize our behaviors, justifying it by saying we needed and deserved this pleasure or someone is being unfair to me to keep me from having what I want. This, coupled with the powerful, reinforcing property of pleasure itself, puts us back in the position of doing it all over again. The cycle repeats itself and we are caught in a process that can occur over and over again.

For some, the needs are so strong and the pleasure is so rewarding that they just skip past the stage in which they feel any guilt and go head-first back into the activity of immediate gratification. This is more likely to occur when there has been a poorly developed, or underutilized, value system in that individual's life, or where a child, growing up was allowed to become self-centered. We are typically not aware of our ego-centric thought patterns because they are seen as appropriate to us and meet our needs. They are not discussed with people who may challenge us, or only discussed with people in our life who agree with our thinking and behavior, and so they become deeply entrenched.

Cycles of Behavior

Thinking and behavior that lead to negative outcomes (and consequences) similar to previous negative outcomes (and consequences) that we have experienced previously may occur rather frequently, or they may be years apart.

These outcomes involve patterns of thinking and behavior that repeat themselves, but often we do not see the repeating patterns occurring. We may explain the negative things that we experience (behaviors and their consequences) as not our fault. We justify our behaviors and the thinking errors behind them as nothing that we can control. The thinking behind our actions and behavior, which turn out to be thinking errors, we have a right to something we want, we are entitled to it, we deserve it, we have earned it somehow and besides, it doesn't hurt anyone to do it.

If anyone questions us or is critical of us, we say they are being unfair to us, and then we may look for other relationships where our thinking and behavior are tolerated or unquestioned (if not welcomed). Such relationships (making friends with people who think the same way we do) are dysfunctional because they either allow us to continue in this negative way, or they encourage the repetition of our behaviors.

New relationships may put off real change. The new person does not know the pattern of our old actions, and so does not question us, but gives us the benefit of the doubt—allowing the cycles of old behavior to start all over again without any real change. Or, if we do try to stay in the relationships we have had, even when things are going wrong, we may try to bargain our way out of it, and say, "I promise, I'll never do that again." It buys time for a while, but then little things happen that we may not see as being important (for example, "I can handle just one drink okay). One drink, then leads to others, and before long we're right back at the same old pattern. We're back in our old "comfort zone" of behaviors where we were before.

It is typical that after having problems or difficulties in our lives (after we experience negative consequences from our actions), we may feel bad or sad for a while and change our behavior primarily because we do feel regret due to the consequences and the loss of things that are important to us). We try to start over with a new plan to change, "I am going to do differently this time," we say, but then, as we saw above, something triggers us, or our past way of thinking and we start all over again.

Searching For The Light

But hopefully, we might indeed say to ourselves, "I commit myself. I am going to change old patterns or find new ways of acting and begin new relationships that will not accept our usual excuses and let us get by with it. We build something new and find new patterns in new situations with a new level of comfort that is without fear or guilt associated with the old behavior and our new path is one of freedom.

This freedom not to return to old patterns of behavior, but to move toward new, healthier, happier patterns means that we have begun to change our "value system", the way we see things and the core values we hold as important in our lives. We may be saying to ourselves, "I'm older, wiser, and have more responsibility now. Besides, I've had enough of the pain and difficulty that my irresponsible behavior from the past has caused. It's over, I want a different life!"

You see, often, when a person has finally had enough negative consequences, they do change. They conclude that what they were doing is not worth the pain that they have caused, so they change because their basic values change. Perhaps it's cheating on a spouse that caused them to lose a marriage, or driving while intoxicated that landed them in jail with lots of financial penalties or the loss of a job. These or other consequences were so severe that finally they created enough chaos and pain that it made the individual want to change.

Ed Wagoner

Before this change occurred perhaps the consequences were not yet severe enough, or a person felt that what they were doing was simply not that bad, so they repeated the behavior enough times until it got worse. Then, suddenly, that individual sees in a totally new way, and can develop a whole new inner set of values that provides long-term change.

Until an individual accepts personal responsibility, the cycles of problematic behavior will continue. The repeating problems may not be the same, but the pattern doesn't really change. Life circumstances may change, but behavior does not until we take charge of our lives not just because we must, but really, because we want to this time. It's up to us.

Chapter X

Steps for Change

Everyone wants a better life. Most people would change if they thought that they would find a better life as a result. Sometimes we feel stuck or at a dead end, but that does not mean we cannot change. You can, if you work for it, can become more successful in life, but that will depend on making good choices and the changes necessary to follow those choices. Success in making fundamental changes in your life depends on six basic steps. If you follow these steps, and work on them as a part of your life, then your life will significantly change, and you will experience success. Not only can you make these changes successfully—we believe that you can—but following them will mean that you feel better about yourself and enjoy succeeding in life. Here they are:

Understanding the Past

The first step is taken when you begin to understanding what has kept you from succeeding in the past. There are many things here to consider, of course, but it is important that you see how you got to where you are now, not so that you can change the past, but so that you can change the present. Here are some things to *consider*:

- What were your early goals for your life? What did you want to accomplish?
- Were any of these goals self-defeating? This means that if you followed them they would land you in some kind of difficulty, and you would be worse off then you were.
- What happened when you followed these goals? How did they turn out?
- What choices did you make back then that affect the present now?
- What is the relationship between the choices you made and the behaviors you used to get what you chose?
- What barriers did these behaviors create around you that affect you as well as others in your life?
- What good role-models were available that helped you early in life, and what role-models that you can see now got you off track?

These are some of the questions you will need to think about and find answers for. Why? Because understanding them will give you insight in how to behave now, and to begin to change some of the behaviors that you have now as a result of your past. The past and the present work together in this way. Understanding the past gives you insight into the present. Here's an example. Let's imagine someone who grew up poor, who did not have many resources. Perhaps that person felt that the "world was against them." That was this person's sense of their past. Let's imagine that the result was this individual wanted to get some of his or her needs met, and so this individual would do things for immediate gratification because they "looked cool," or because other role-models did them and seemed to get what they wanted. This pattern of behavior, of course, would lead to a cycle of choices and actions that often spiraled into more and more self-defeating behavior. Now, your life may not have been exactly like this. For example, you may not have grown up poor, but for other reasons you began to make bad choices and added to the cycle by the behaviors you chose.

Believing in Yourself

Everyone makes mistakes. Sometimes very bad mistakes, but people can recover from them, but only if they start believing in themselves again— believing that they are not fundamentally a bad person, but a good person who has made bad choices. By believing in yourself again, that you are a good person who can change and make new choices that will help you succeed, you lay the foundation for a new life.

Every person experiences failure in life. Sometimes failures come at great cost to you. You lose much, more than you ever imagined, but you

Ed Wagoner

manage to struggle through and survive somehow. The question is, what do you do to start over again—learning from the mistakes and failures you have experienced along the way? You have options open to you at every point. You can take these options and start a new path, but what are they?

The first is that you need to understand something about the mistakes and failures themselves. It may not actually be you who failed, but the decision you made along the way that led to failure. The point is, that most people want to do what's right, but not knowing fully what is up ahead, or not seeing completely the whole picture, they make decisions based upon only a part of the picture, or upon faulty information or beliefs about themselves or the situation, and the result is a significant setback. The fact is that a person, given better information and better beliefs could make better decisions. That is true of you as well. The more you know, the better your information, the better your decisions will be in the future. You can make new decisions that will lead to success in life.

Here is a key in making good decisions: ask yourself, what is realistic and what is fantasy? For example, you say, "Well, I want to become president of a large company," but you have no experience in business, or "I want to be rich in five years," but you don't have a good job you can actually do, or any new skills for a new job. You may need to do some soul-searching here. You may be trying to take steps that are too large, or you may be taking no real steps at all. So we each have to learn what our options are. What are realistic options, and then actually do them. This means that we have to believe in ourselves enough to make the adjustments, do some planning, and take the necessary steps toward a future in which success is possible. So you have to start with realistic goals—maybe "small steps" at first, and accomplish these before you take longer and larger steps. Each "baby step" will lead to new possibilities, and you can build one upon the other.

For example, you want to have a better life and more money so that you don't always feel like you are making no financial progress. What are your options? Perhaps the next step is asking, "What could I learn to do that is available to me?" Maybe you could start with some new training, or perhaps you could start looking for a job that pays better wages, and so you get "on site" training in a new job. These are realistic goals, and they lead to better pay, more money, and yes, perhaps, being wealthier in the future. But you can't have more wealth, if you don't start out being realistic, and taking the first small steps toward your goal. Each step is a success, and you are being successful because you believe in yourself, understanding your options realistically, making good new choices, and successfully taking those first small steps in a new direction.

Ed Wagoner

Motivation to Make the Changes Stick

The third step is about being motivated enough to make the changes you are making stick because they are a priority in your life. You care about your life, and you care enough about yourself to stick with the new choices you have made. You see that it is going to be a long-term commitment because the goal includes the rest of your life. This is not an easy "quick fix" that will gratify immediate needs, but in the end it will get you were you need to go. So now you are motivated to stick with the plan and make the changes happen over a longer period of time.

The motivation for this long-term effort comes not from someone making you do it outside yourself, but from you reinforcing yourself from within. If you are seeing progress and if you are having successes all along the way, then you will be motivated, because you will be motivating yourself. But success, of course, comes one small step at a time. If we think that we are going to make some huge leap of progress in a short time, we will be disappointed. But if we realize that success means lots of small steps, we will have the belief, "I'm really making progress. It may be slow, but it is progress."

The problem with expecting "big things right of the bat" is that we will certainly start with a sense of motivation, but if the "big things" don't quite materialize, then we lose commitment, and start to forget about out good decisions and our long-term goals. We need to keep a steady commitment, and that means planning for those small steps all along the way. So how do we do that?

Well, let's take the problem we want to solve, or the goal we want to reach first, and just look at it. Study it awhile. Think about, what is required here? If I want to solve this, or reach my goal, what are the steps I need to take right at the beginning, then what is next, and then, more planning—what more do I need? I might need to make a list of the long-term plan (where I start, and where do I want to end or see happen) and what are the steps that I need to take all along the way? Now every plan is just that, a plan. It can be changed. It's not in concrete, but because you see what needs to be done in small pieces, you can take each one and work on it till you are ready for the next one, that way you have both the big picture in mind as well as the pieces that make up the whole picture.

For example, let's say you want a new job, and maybe you even apply for one and get turned down. Well, is the "game over," your defeated and there is nothing else to do? No, not achieving the first time is just the start. Keep working on it. Perseverance is a wonderful characteristic of successful people. You hear lots of stories about people who were eventually successful and achieved their goals, but who felt that they failed over and over again all along the way. The key

Ed Wagoner

thing is that until they found the right doorway they never gave up. You see success is always a long-term goal and everything you do toward that goal is progress, even though you may not have quite reached it yet. Working on it, and in the process, working on you is already a great achievement.

You must remember the saying, "When at first you don't succeed, try, and try again!" You may not achieve your goal, or solve your problem the first time you try, but you've already learned a lot. Success is a long-term progress and it means never giving up even when you don't achieve what you want in the short-term. It is the long-term that you are after.

Believing that you can accomplish what you want, and never giving up, though you are quite aware that it won't be easy is being successful already. Everyone experiences set-backs. When you experience a challenge, know that everyone who has ever made progress has had to work through lots of challenges and setbacks, but the key was they still didn't give up.

Often at this point people begin to feel bad. They slack off. Something inside their heads starts saying, "See you really are a failure," or "This proves it, you really are a weak person, you might as well give up." But that inner voice is wrong on both counts. You are not a weak person because you failed at something. It's only a test, a challenge, and let's see what you can do with it now. Again, perhaps you've only been looking at the big picture, and not the smaller steps along the way. So now instead of backing off, take another smaller step.

What you need to ask yourself at that moment is, "So what do I do next? What can I do now? Do I need to look in another direction or for a solution I haven't even thought of?" Perhaps you need to talk to someone who you know has achieved the goals you want, and see what they have to say. They may give you some really good new insight and point you in new directions that had never come into your mind. Start thinking positively instead of negatively. Capitalize on the positive things you already know or have, and add to what you don't have one step at a time. You may need to develop some new skills for yourself. Maybe you need to learn how to talk to people better, or what to say in a certain circumstances. Get some help on this. Don't always work alone.

Learning New Skills, Thinking, and Behaviors

No change can happen by doing the same old thing and expecting new results. To get new results, you will have to learn new skills; new ways of thinking, and of course, new ways of acting that can take you in a positive direction. You can teach an old dog new tricks, that is, if they are motivated to learn. But old patterns do die hard, and this learning will take time and work.

Ed Wagoner

We already saw that we had to start planning ahead. In your planning for the future you must make room for a learning process. Ask yourself what do I need to know that I don't know at this time in order to get where I need to go? Where I can find the right person, or the right way to learn what I need to learn? Just asking those questions is progress, and it is even better when you start searching for answers.

So let's begin. Learning new skills might mean, first of all, that you have to "unlearn" some old behavior and ways of thinking before you can actually find new ones. You see it is easy to develop behaviors or thoughts about life or yourself based on too little information. For example, when you were younger during childhood, you might have begun to think about yourself or what you wanted based on information that was incomplete or incorrect. Like most children, you were too young to really evaluate what was good for you and what was not, or what would help you in life and what would hinder you later. Some of the things you may have thought turned out, in the end, to diminish your life. So you may have to evaluate the way you think about yourself, or the way you behave and see if it is helping or hurting you now. Think about this for awhile. Study it, and see what you can find out about the following questions. These will help you to understand and find new answers:

Searching For The Light

How did you learn to meet your needs as a child? What sorts of experiences did you go through to get your needs met when you were young? For example you may have met your needs by being very demanding with your parents, or by being secretive and deceptive. If so, why was it so important to get your needs met in this way? It is probably true that you really didn't know how to get things done the way you wanted, but you experimented and whatever brought you success, you did. Each time you were successful, even if it was doing something negative, it reinforced your sense of at least being rewarded. It may have made you feel better or less afraid. Perhaps you were drawn to and encouraged by a set of friends that did the same thing or felt the same way you did. You may have started drinking or doing drugs or hanging out with the wrong sort of friends, but something happened to make you feel you needed to do better.

Other people who didn't get into trouble the way you may have, used sports, or some hobby, or going to work, or forming healthy relationships to get positive feedback and reinforcement. We all used something, and some things led to one path and some to another, but it is important to understand the path that we took and how we got from where we started to where we are now. Think about it. See if you can trace your path from your childhood till now. Look carefully at what decisions you made for good or for bad along the way. Can you identify a point where you maybe

Ed Wagoner

began to get off track: being deceptive or aggressive, or getting attention, even if it was negative?

Maybe it was only in adulthood that you began to see that at work or in marriage the ways you learned to act early on or the "skills" you have been using don't really work so well any more. Perhaps, as a result, you lost your marriage or your job, for example. It is clear, then that you need to learn new skills. Perhaps you are not even sure what those may be. You're at a bit of a loss and at a crossroads as well.

As you examine yourself and your life, you may see that you do not understand yourself very well. You may need to discover what you really want out of life now, what you enjoy, what you want to become, and what motivates you. Or you may see that you need to develop new thinking skills that will help you see things in a new way. You may need new ways to think about yourself and your life. You may also see that you need to think more positively about things (yourself or your life). Or you may need to listen to the people, who care about you, or to act in more appropriate ways, or learn how to present yourself so that others think positively of you without being too defensive, too shy, or too aggressive.

These are some suggestions, but they may not be what are important right now for you, or they may be. You need to decide for yourself what new skill you want to learn next from these or from something else important to your life. Make a decision, and then work through the following list as helpful suggestions in your desire to learn.

- Do some reading about the area you most want to work on.
- See what information is already out there and available to you.
- Make a list of requirements for learning this new skill.
- Find out what new responsibilities you will need to pick up for learning this new skill—what is required of you if you move in this direction.
- Go talk to people who have learned this skill or done what you want to accomplish. What do they think about it? What advice would they give you? How could they help you achieve your goal?
- Find out about the financial requirements or the financial benefits for taking this next step.
- Start a file of material and arrange in it the order that will help you most.

Abandon Old Behavior and Thinking and Make the Right Choices

This plan will never work if you do not take what you have learned—the new skills, the new thinking and the new behavior—and actually do them. The fact is you don't know if what you have learned is actually a new skill until you are able to put it into practice. This means, of course, that you have to let go of the old and the familiar patterns that caused you not to be successful in life in the first place, and choose the new over the old and "just do it."

We move into a new way of life by leaving off old patterns and accomplishing the new. Remember, if you keep on doing what you have always done, you'll keep on getting the same old results. Albert Einstein's interesting definition of craziness is to keep doing what you have always done, but expect different results. It rarely, if ever, happens. So if you leave the old patterns and begin new ones, you will inevitably see new results. It may take awhile, but the truth is, things are going to change, that is, if you are persistent and keep doing what you need to do.

One of the best ways to begin the change process is to re-evaluate who you hang out with—your friends. You may be friendly with a lot of people, but the question always is, not are your friends friendly, but do they help you toward a better life? You want to know if your friends are really a positive force in your life, or are they enabling you to negative behaviors? If you decide they are a negative force in your life, then even if they are "friendly" their friendship is reducing the benefit. Friendship is even better if it is from people whose lives are also, like you, moving in a positive direction and helping you to do the same.

Searching For The Light

Often we discover that we have dysfunctional relationships with people that tear us down instead of build us up. It may be hard to change those relationships immediately, but we need to start and follow through until we have a different set of relationships that help rather than hinder us.

Another important issue in all of this is that true change does not come from outside yourself. Even reading this page, if it is not something you want to do inside yourself, it won't really help you very much. But if you really want to change, then change will happen, because the motivation for it is inside of you. This is internal vs. external reinforcement. If you are finding pleasure in a new way of life, and enjoy living in a positive way, then you will have the motivation to keep on going, and you will also begin to influence others around you. When I can see my life is moving along in a new direction, then I begin to realize a new way of life and have real insight into who I am and what I want in life both now and in the future.

All that we have said so far involves something that we might call a value system. Every person, whether they know it or not have a core set of beliefs and principles that they hold inside. Maybe even without fully realizing it, or being able to describe it, they live those principles. This is called accepting the Social Contract. These core beliefs help to shape your life and the direction you take in life because they are the "real you."

Ed Wagoner

Core values need not be "big things," they can be such simple things as the pure enjoyment of being relaxed and at peace, talking with good friends, and getting away from stress and being in nature. These can be a person's deep, core values, and developing an inner set of core values can help replace old actions with the new and then go on to balance the new behaviors with activities that provide both pleasure while maintaining daily responsibilities. Your core values will help you, for example, put responsibilities to yourself and your family ahead pure personal pleasure or selfish desires, but in the end they will strengthen even these. They will also help you face difficult times and give you strength to move through them. They will also let you block (or set aside) errors in your thinking and judgment that take you in the wrong direction, because a better direction in life is what you really deserve.

Sometimes it is easier to see these core values (either negative or positive) in someone else. For example, positively, you may be able see them in another person who is more at peace and whose life is more fulfilling than your own. By watching you can see your own behavior reflected or compared with theirs. You can also see what new decisions about the way you live and changes in the way you behave you may need to make. All of this gives you insight that you can really use.

Or to take a negative example, you may see that for some people the desire for selfish pleasure is often stronger than the pain of the consequences and the results are often harmful. For example people who get DUI's or busted for drugs, or can't hold a job. When you see this lived out in someone else who has to go through it, you can learn to avoid it in your life or in yourself. No matter how difficult it may be to make the necessary changes, you can say, "I am not going to quit now because it is ultimately in my best interest to make the changes because I deserve a better life, one without negative consequences and further pain. Only I can decide that and what I will do about it. The good thing is, I am free to make these changes, and no one is forcing me.

Constantly Use Your New Knowledge to Your Advantage In the end it is the continual practice and use of these new skills that will increase your success. So the final step is to constantly use your new knowledge and skills to make responsible, healthy choices which will bring about successful changes in your life. Each step you take on this path will give you more control over your own future and where your life is going. Ultimately these steps will bring peace to your life. This has been the goal all along, and it is worth all the effort and the sacrifices you have made, and continue to make, as you move forward.

So, how do you live and practice this last step? Here are some important pointers. First, you have to begin by practicing it on a day-to-day basis, just the way you normally live. You have to get up

Ed Wagoner

each day and make a commitment to yourself to be responsible, to do what will make your life better that day. Second, this means that you will also have to be patient and tolerant with yourself for you are, as we all are, an imperfect creature and life is never perfect. But as best you can, you must steadily keeping the possibility of "back-tracking" or moving backwards "at bay" as you move forward. Third, you have to learn to manage the challenges of life without getting bogged down in the anger or the resentments that you may feel. Fourth, in addition, you must practice better and better communication skills with others and learn to listen to others with more attentiveness.

As we learn these basic skills, we can then pay closer attention to the results of each of them and see how this is new way of being and behaving provides a much better way of life for us in comparison to the experiences and outcomes we had in the past. Seeing this helps to reinforce our new way of living since we realize the beneficial results these changes are making in our lives and why such changes are worth it.

For example, the better I feel about the way I am living now the less fear and anxiety have to deal with. As problems arise (even setbacks), I can think them through more clearly and see how to proceed forward or what I would do better the next time. If I see that indeed I could have handled a difficult situation better, I can better understand what the results might have been had I done differently? At each step I am thinking more clearly and learning as I go. Indeed, I am learning all the time.

Let's imagine I didn't like or enjoy a particular situation that came up in my life, but also, to my credit, I didn't escalate the situation into a new conflict. I kept my cool and didn't retaliate. When it is all over there is nothing to apologize for. Even if it was difficult, and it left me with some bad feelings, I came out better in the end because I didn't have to go into a "mop up operation" to fix the mess I might have made otherwise.

In this way, in the circumstances that arise in life I can begin to have a sense of control over my life. These also help me to evaluate the relationships I currently have more clearly. If I am being fair with others I can see whether or not people are being fair and reasonable with me. I can see whether or not I am being treated well. This allows me to evaluate my situation and make clearer decisions about where I want to go in any future relationships I have because I can see better without the fog of my own "out-of-control emotions" blocking my view.

In that regard, I can also evaluate my relationships on the job and where I think my work is taking me. Perhaps I do need a new job, perhaps not, but I can now make changes wisely. This brings about stability and peace and keeps me moving forward. Too much conflict would have

Ed Wagoner

kept me from seeing and evaluating things that clearly or objectively.

Like every human being, I deserve to be at peace and to have a measure of happiness and contentment in life. I need people to treat me well when I act responsibly. By controlling my own behavior and acting responsibly, not only have I earned this new kind of life, I deserve it—but I also keep working at it. This journey to a better life is never at an end.

Chapter XI

Anger Management

There is probably not a person alive who has not felt anger and even rage at some time in his or her life. It is part of our human emotions, and sometimes it appears fairly regularly, especially in a world that often seems to challenge us and go against what we want or feel. If you take a look at the animal world and then at humans, it is clear that we exist on earth because we have learned to survive in what appears to be a very dangerous environment at times. In order to survive, we and the other creatures have either had to stand and fight or run away to escape the danger. This is called the "fight or flight strategy for survival." It appears to be built right into us. When we are threatened, we use either one of these two possibilities almost automatically. If we are confronted with something that is a threat and we feel that it is putting us at risk, we will either become aggressive, or we will try to escape and get away from it. Another possibility is to do nothing, remain passive. These options may lead to a negative outcome.

Here are some things we need to know. First, anger is a normal part of a human being. It is natural in animals as well. We see it everywhere, both around and inside of us. We learn how to express anger in the very process of growing up. At an early age we begin to develop independence from our mother—the primary care giver. We are

Ed Wagoner

learning to be a unique individual, and we begin to experience what that means. An infant will early on start to engage the environment that he or she is in to get basic needs met. For example, a child will cry so that he or she can be fed, or needs attention. As that child grows he or she may become more demanding, cry louder or longer, or even begin to scream. It is then that a parent must start to teach limits. A mother can let a child cry for awhile without immediately jumping up to stop the crying. This is not a bad thing, but a way to help a child to manage their feelings and put limits on their behavior.

Later a child may exaggerate his or her wants and desires by becoming even more demanding—by throwing a fit, expressing temper and even getting "physical" (hitting out or biting) in order to get his or her way. Here is a set of behaviors that if left uncontrolled or unmanaged can get out of hand and become a very troubling habit. A parent must stop the physical aggression, and control the outburst in a responsible manner, or the chaos around the child will only grow and become worse. I like to use the term benevolent authoritarian to describe the parenting style I recommend. We have all experienced "spoiled children" whose parents put no controls on this behavior. The consequences are that the child may get their immediate needs met in this way, but people in the world around them will start to react in negative ways, and the spiral of anger, aggression, and temper will grow until someone, somewhere begins to put a stop to it—and others, for example a relative, or a teacher, will attempt to socialize a child and manage the anger in a new way. If a child isn't taught limits to anger, temper, and aggressive behavior and isn't taught any early anger management skills, and if the child is simply allowed to continue using anger as a way to meet needs on through life, and then obviously as the challenges grow, the behavior becomes more and more aggressive. Often the force necessary to stop it also grows, and eventually the community' or possibly the law gets involved and the person who never learned anger management ends up in an environment where someone else (the justice system, for example) is in control.

So you can see, that from childhood when we are under pressure or are angry, it is easy to simply "let it out," and our anger can spill everywhere almost uncontrollably. But when it does, as an adult we will probably have to pick up some pieces and may lose someone or something important to us. More important than the survival technique of fighting or fleeing, is the need to use social skills. Cooperation trumps anger or escape as the most important survival skill on the planet. We see it in operation everywhere. Animals learn to cooperate with each other to make a balanced ecology. Humans learn to cooperate in order to have a safe environment in which to live and raise their children. If aggressive people were in charge of everything, then life would be chaotic, unsafe, and the balances of the world would collapse.

Ed Wagoner

Look at what happened to past dictators. (Hitler for example) Yes, we experience anger—and sometimes it is necessary and can serve as a motivator for change, but usually that survival part of us must be managed by a higher principle. So let us look at anger, and how we can learn to manage it and create a world that is safe and balanced for us to live in.

One of the results that come from cooperation is building a support system. A support system is a group of people you have around you that are willing to help you in meeting your day to day needs, your family, friends, and community. You are a part of that support system by helping all of the people in your support system meet their day to day needs. The bigger your support system the more secure you are. You may need a ride to work or school; you may need a short term loan, someone to take care of you when you're sick. No man is an island and the more people we have in our support system the higher functioning we are going to be. This is the primary reason we must learn to accept the social contract. (More on this later)

Conflict Resolution

There are few people who are in some sort of relationship that don't experience conflict. It's just the way it is—and this is true in friendships as well and most other important relationships, such as working relationships. Conflicts inevitably develop. We become angry at our parent, significant other, friend, co-worker, boss, etc. We have to learn to handle conflicts, and look for ways of managing them that will give us a better outcome than letting disagreements destroying the relationship. So what's the answer? How can we learn to manage conflicts in our lives and relationships?

We need to be assertive with our concerns and not try to hide them or ignore them. We must learn to stand up for ourselves assertively and speak or say what we feel, but when we do we must learn also to avoid a fight. The very best thing to do in speaking up for yourself and yet avoiding a fight is to try to not speak when we are overwhelmed with emotion. We need to allow everyone time to calm down. We have arrange it so that we come to the conflict (and speak about it) in a more neutral environment than we might do otherwise when something is really bothering us.

But before we arrange to say anything to the person we are having some difficulty with, we have to decide—is this really an important issue? Is this the issue and the place on which I want to spend emotional capital and energy? If it is, then you need to think and prepare what you are going to say, and not just blurt out something that you might regret later. What do you want to say to that person that is really important? What do you need to say? What must be said? What should be left out? And just as important, how do you want to say it? Make a plan, and then carry it out it when you are not angry and in emotional turmoil—but more calm and at peace.

When you do sit down, to talk, don't find fault or blame the other person for the perceived problem. That approach won't help much at all. In fact, it will only make the person you're really trying to communicate with more defensive and less likely to hear what you want to say. Instead, talk about the issue and how it affects you, not what they did to create the problem, and how bad or at fault they are. Then, of course, you want to work toward some solution that, if at all possible, will be good for both parties involved—fair to both sides, so that both of you get something good out of it. To achieve this, you must be willing to compromise. Ask yourself, "What would I be willing to live with that may not be perfect, but would be better than what I have now?"

What this will mean of course, is that you need to approach this conversation in a business like way—the way you would if you were talking to an associate at work, perhaps—in a much more neutral and less emotional way. Even when you are in a difficult situation emotionally, do it with this sense of greater neutrality, more objectively. Talk about what your needs are, and how it affects you. Talk about your feelings, and ask the other person to be as open as possible about his or her feelings without becoming defensive. Talk about what your rights are as individuals, and the respect that is required of each other to help maintain those rights.

Remember, if you are going to be open with each other, then you have to be willing to deal with constructive criticism from the other person. The other person has feelings just like you do, and perhaps emotional feelings. You must express all of this without belittling each other. Finding a solution in this kind of open environment will mean that you each must be flexible and discuss options. It will be important to discuss each person's ideas and perspectives when you have this meeting.

Focus: on how a situation or another person's behavior affects you and how you can deal with it in a fair and objective way that is good for both parties.

Using Aggressive Behavior When Angry

- Aggression is an easy way to deal with feelings of insecurity and the sense of inadequacy.
- When angry there is the tendency is to demean the character of another person.
- To say something to bring someone back in control.
- Deflate the sense of self worth of another person, implying that they are not a worthy person or adversary.

Ed Wagoner

Resolving Anger Issues

- Try to resolve the conflict and avoid aggressive behavior.
- Treat the other person with respect even in a conflict.
- If you have empathy for another person you will try to understand the other person's point of view. Ask: "How do you see the problem we are having?"
- Listen to the other side. Respond: "Here's the problem as I see it."
- Open the door to further communication and negotiation: "Here is a solution from my perspective. How do you see it?"
- Strive for a win-win solution.
- Possible way forward: "Here's a solution for both of us."
- These are tools to achieve a much better end (resolution) rather than using aggression.

Learning a New Skill

- Anger is a normal, natural response to feelings of frustration. It can be healthy if we use its energy to motivate us to learn new skills and behaviors.
- In a conflict these feelings have to be managed. Emotion can be the first thing we experience, and therefore, must be dealt with.

- It is a myth that "anger is not controllable." It is controllable. For example: if you are around someone with more power than you, no matter what happens you will most likely control your anger. (Because you don't want to experience some consequence, I.E. get fired, or get into an argument).
- You must understand that you have other tools, and if you learn to use those tools, in time, anger will not be your first response.
- First, you must learn not to let other people "push your buttons." Take time to get your thoughts together before you react.
- Second, do not let our emotions or another person's emotional state prevent us from being objective, or from using good verbal interactions (calmly discussing issues) to resolve the conflict.
- Third, understand the things in your life that have contributed to aggressive behavior. (anger, jealousy, hurt feelings, substance use, etc)
- Fourth, often, instead of using aggressive behavior, sometimes an individual will use passive-aggressive behavior as a response. We must understand how to recognize this type of behavior.

Ed Wagoner

Passive-Aggressive Behavior

- Passive aggressive behavior may be defined in a number of ways. First, as a failure to cooperate, to either consciously or unconsciously become uncooperative. Second, a form of resistance that resorts to manipulation and deception in getting what one wants. This eventually creates problems for others and makes the resolution of conflict difficult.
- When an individual becomes intimidated and yet does not openly confront the conflict, the result is often to repress anger and aggressiveness which can often become "free floating" and is expressed in subtle ways beyond the originating situation.
- It is easy for free floating anger to be expressed in another situation or toward individuals who are not directly involved, but may be easier targets to express the repressed feelings that an individual may have.
- Individuals who use passive-aggression either consciously or unconsciously may be experiencing signs of poor self-esteem. They have allowed other people to take control of their power or life. They have allowed someone to manipulate them because the individual does not have the skills or the knowledge to be self-assertive.

- The individual, as a result, does not feel good about him or herself. Passive-aggressive behavior, therefore, is an easy way to deal both with the feelings of insecurity and the sense of being overwhelmed.
- This individual interferes with other people in such a way that it becomes disruptive, or it sabotages relationships and situations creating conflict and confusion. This may be subliminal in nature, and not even in the consciousness of the individual who is doing it.
- The deep sense is: "I'm not going to do what they want me to do." On the surface it may appear that there is compliance and cooperation, but underneath there is covert, non-cooperative resistance.

Assertiveness

- Assertiveness helps an individual build a sense of self-esteem because that person can authentically express his or her true feelings. . I.E. No I don't want to do that, or make that decision right now. It gives you time to think things over, make the best choice.
- You speak directly in a calm manner, about how a person or situation affects you, makes you feel. You describe the behavior that the other person is doing objectively. State what you feel needs to

Ed Wagoner

happen in everyone's best interest. Speak in I terms, not you terms without name calling or blame. It allows you to exercise your personal choice. It makes it possible for a person to become more effective in dealing with the normal conflicts that arise in the course of daily life. Assertiveness gives you the skill and patience to deal with frustrating people and situations.

- Assertiveness can result in a win-win situation that is constructive rather than destructive to relationships and complex situations. Assertiveness is one of the best skills you can learn. There are numerous books and articles on assertiveness online. It will benefit you a great deal to learn more.

A mother once asked a trusted teacher;
When she should begin the education of her child.
"How old is she?" asked the teacher.
"She's five."
"Five! Hurry home!
You're five years late already!"

Anger is like a blazing flame that burns up our self-control,
and causes us to say and do thing that we regret later.

Searching For The Light

Thich Nhat Hanh

Remember, anger is an emotion,
and emotions seldom successfully solve problems.
Instead, they may be more likely to create new ones.
John Marks Templeton

Anger is just one letter short of danger.

Anger and hatred are the materials from which hell is made.
Thich Nhat Hanh

Anger is a momentary madness,
so control your passion or it will control you.
Horace

Ed Wagoner

Chapter XII

Autonomy and Empathy

We each grew up in families, some of which were healthy and some, we realize, may not have been as healthy. We talk about families as "healthy" because they help us to function well on our own, in society, and as human beings who make a good contribution to the world. We talk about unhealthy families as dysfunctional, because they make it more difficult for people to function well as human beings on their own, in society, or are unable to contribute to our Family and Community.

Something important that healthy families do is making it possible for a child growing up in them to become independent (or autonomous) and to have empathy for others. These two important characteristics work together in an interesting way. A person growing up in a healthy family learns from those around him or her to feel good about themselves. In a healthy family the parents reinforce the fact that their child is a good person, and as a result, that individual begins to develop a sense of self-respect. The child feels that they are valuable because they are valued and important. The result is that they feel that they have a sense of control over their lives and can therefore be independent and experience autonomy as a person.

You might think that an independent, autonomous person would be self-centered—

concerned only about his or herself, but the opposite is true. An individual who is truly autonomous is someone that knows and practices the fact that everyone has the same rights to independence and freedom that he or she has. This allows that person to have care and empathy for others. An autonomous person offers the same respect to others that he or she enjoys, and treats others just and he or she wishes to be treated.

A person who has a sense of self-worth and autonomy is someone who not only feels good about him or herself, but is also a person who is fair, just, reasonable, and honest with others. These are, of course, values that make you (or anyone) a well-adjusted person with strength of character, and the ability to function well on your own, in society, and to make a contribution to the environment as well.

An interesting thing about such a person is that they are strong enough, and feel good enough about themselves not to allow negative influences to change who they are or their fundamental direction in life. They can stay steady in the face of pressure or challenges. They are not easily tempted or turned in a direction that they know is going to have a negative effect or outcome. They have a sense of inner strength to meet negativity and challenges. They are wiser in that regard. Why is this so? The answer is that autonomy (being independent and feeling good about you) gives an individual a personal sense of security. That

Ed Wagoner

person not only knows who they are, but they also know the difference between right and wrong, and how to work with what is right and avoid what is wrong. They know, also, how to be empathetic with others because they can understand the hurt and pain that others feel, and also, how their own behavior may or may not contribute pain or harm. They care about what happens to others.

This ability to feel the pain of others is something, perhaps, that we may inherit from birth. If we live in a healthy environment, then that ability will grow and strengthen. If, however, we grow up in a world where there is fear, and where we feel threatened or in danger in some way, or are in pain ourselves because we are made to feel like we were of little or no value, or less than a good person, then that ability may change, be suppressed or diminished, or even be turned into its opposite. As he or she grows up, every human person has a "window of opportunity" to develop autonomy and empathy. Everyone has that same window, but the question is, of course, has the environment around that individual been healthy enough that these natural tendencies can grow and flourish so that an individual in later life can develop social responsibility.

In this kind of environment empathy toward others may seem more difficult because the world a person lived in was so difficult, dangerous, or fearful that they spent all their early energies and time trying to take care of themselves, just to survive. However, it must be said, even in those exceptions where people grow up under difficult circumstances, many individuals emerge with the ability for autonomy and empathy—they manage to overcome those difficulties. Many adults, later on in life, who grew up in those same difficult circumstances and were negatively affected by them, also begin to overcome these influences and become autonomous, caring, empathetic human beings. There is hope for everyone, no matter where they started or who they are.

<blockquote>
The one who is full of himself
is likely to be quite empty.
Unknown Author
</blockquote>

<blockquote>
A conceited man has a swelling head
and a shrinking brain.
Unknown Author
</blockquote>

<blockquote>
The hallmark of courage in our age of conformity
is the capacity to stand on one's convictions—
not obstinately or defiantly
(These are gestures of defensiveness, not courage)
Nor as a gesture of retaliation,
But simply because these are what one believes.
--*Rollo May*
</blockquote>

Ed Wagoner

You are what you are
By what you believe.
--*Oprah Winfrey*

The only real satisfaction there is,
is to be growing up inwardly all the time,
becoming more just, true, generous, simple,
manly, womanly, kind, active.
And this we can all do,
by doing each day the day's work as well as we can.
--*James Freeman Clarke*

Do all the good you can,
By all the means you can,
In all the places you can,
To all the people you can,
As long as ever you can.
--*John Wesley*

Chapter XIII

Self-Concept and Self-Esteem

At the core of whom and what we are is something very deep. It is called our sense of self, or some call it our "self-concept", our "ego." This means that we each have a feel for whom and what we are and that we carry this sense around inside us. That self-sense becomes the basis for what we are and what we do in the world. We behave, speak, act, and respond to others based on the way we see ourselves.

Related to our own self-concept is something even deeper and that is self-esteem. We have a sense of ourselves, but the question is what do we think about ourselves? How do we evaluate ourselves? Do we value ourselves, or do we discount and undervalue ourselves and perhaps hold ourselves, strangely, at some distance? Some people do not even really like themselves; you suspect this because they become self-destructive. In subtle or not-so-subtle ways they subvert themselves, creating a world of chaos and confusion that eventually destroys the self they are. This sense of self-esteem is often difficult to talk about, because it is so close to us. Perhaps we even "keep it a secret" from our normal, waking, thinking mind.

If someone were to say casually, "Do you like yourself?" We would probably reply that we do—at least most of the time. But that might still not

Ed Wagoner

tell us much about our own sense of ourselves and the deeper issues of self-esteem, the value that we put on ourselves.

If we really like ourselves then we will behave one way. If we do not like ourselves, or have a mixed feeling about ourselves, we will behave in a completely different way. This is an important insight into understanding ourselves as we move forward in this work. Our self-concept and our sense of self-esteem will determine almost everything else about us, what we do, how we think, and how we respond to others. What is interesting is that we can change this aspect of ourselves. Our sense of self-esteem can be strengthened. Our self-concept can be changed. We can come to see and feel differently about ourselves. Like everything else, we can grow and mature here as well. We can also change our self-esteem. We can come gradually to really value who we are, and think better about ourselves if we have lived with a lower sense of esteem.

This understanding is important for many reasons, but one that is central to our work is this. If we have a good self-sense, meaning we understand who we are and what we stand for, and our sense of self-esteem is high, then we will take better care of ourselves using values we know we can trust. If our self-sense is weak, and our self-esteem is low, then we will be unclear about and less committed to our own set of values and more likely to be persuaded to use someone else's untested values which can get us into trouble. If we are more susceptible to values other than our own, and more open to allowing others to sway us to their own values which may or may not be good for us, then we will not choose clearly the better path. If we pair our thinking and behavior with the values we know are beyond question, we will feel valuable and have a good self concept.

>Self-worth cannot be verified by others.
>You are worthy because you say it is so.
>If you depend on others for your value
>it is other-worth.
>*Wayne Dyer*

>The happiest people don't necessarily have the best of everything;
>They just make the best of everything they have.
>Unknown Author

>The deepest principle in human nature
>Is the craving to be appreciated?
>*William James*

>Complaining about yourself is a useless activity,
>and one which keeps you from effectively living your life.
>It encourages self-pity and immobilizes you in your efforts
>at giving and receiving love.

Ed Wagoner

Wayne Dyer

To be truly human means to choose your true self.
Everything you decide makes you be in a certain way.
It builds your life in a certain direction.
This is true of your decision regarding **what** to do.
It is also true of your decision regarding **how** to do it.
Your life situation may have imposed on you already what you should do.
One thing remains up to you always
and that **how** to **uniquely** do what you are doing.
Adrian Van Kaam

Self-love means accepting yourself as a worthy person
Because you choose to do so.
Wayne Dyer

Chapter Fourteen

Needs and Relationships

When we build relationships where there is an effort to meet a need in either partner. The new relationship we seek has the potential for dysfunction. To understand this dynamic we first need to define neediness. Neediness is an inner state in which a person feels insecure because he or she is lacking something, is incomplete in some way, or feels a deep sense of deficit. This may be due in part because along the way, as a person grew up, some ingredient that was essential for healthy relationships was not present or was often lacking.

For example, at a certain stage of growth when a person needed unconditional love from a parent or from the family, it was seldom, or perhaps, never there, and so that person potentially grew up with a deficit in being loved. As a result that individual may be needy, always be seeking to fill that void by getting other people to be with them to fill that sense of emptiness or need. A person may become excessively dependent on others, or suppress their own feelings in a relationship out of the fear of being alone, or allow others to mistreat them simply because they feel the need to be in a relationship. This person has what we might call a "need-deficit," and is trying to fill that personal need by being involved with someone else who will meet it for them.

Ed Wagoner

The question is, in a relationship, do they "have to have this other person" or something from this other person to feel good about their self? If the answer is "yes," then as the relationship develops, they probably will not be building it on a solid foundation.

So to avoid this problem, they need to take time understanding not only another person, but their own motives for being in relationship. They should not get into a relationship prematurely without taking time to let it grow, and allowing them to understand all the dynamics that might be involved—especially the "hidden ones" that might not be apparent immediately.

Most importantly, as a relationship grows, each partner needs to maintain certain healthy boundaries and standards that do not compromise the values and sense of self-esteem that the separate individuals must have to be in a strong and mature relationship. Such individuals, then, will not use the other person and try to fill the "holes" in their lives. Holes in our lives can only be healed from within (by the personal work we do with them), and not from without. When we allow the "holes" within (the lacks and deficits we feel), to go unattended to, then they have the potential for creating problems in a relationship. They interfere by creating this dynamic of neediness, and in the long run these inner insecurities and problems end up hurting the very relationships that are most important.

Searching For The Light

Finding and Holding Long-term relationships

Many people discover that it is difficult to find and hold on to a good relationship. Why is this so? There are many factors involved, of course, in finding good relationships. The first factor is that finding a relationship actually it starts with you, the person who is looking for a good, steady relationship, and not with the other person you are looking for. First you have to know yourself, and be in a good place before you can find someone who is also in a good place. If you start looking when you are in a bad place, when you are feeling alone, perhaps a little insecure, you will probably end up with something that will not be either stable or satisfying.

So the search for a good relationship begins with you. Before you begin looking for a relationship with someone who will be significant in your life, you must ask yourself, "Am I in a good place right now? Am I in a state of equilibrium and balance—feeling good about myself so that I can start a relationship with someone else?" Or, "Am I in a state of instability? Am I feeling a need, too motivated to be in a relationship?" If the answer is "yes," to these questions, then before you begin, you need to do some work with yourself—perhaps you need to talk to someone (a trusted friend, a counselor, or pastor, for example), and get a handle on why you

Ed Wagoner

are feeling this way, so that you can move into some new place where you are feeling better, steady and more secure. Never begin a relationship when you are feeling bad about yourself, unsteady and missing something because you are likely to make choices about another person for the wrong reasons.

You have to realize that this happens when most people try hard to find a new relationship in the hopes that someone or something outside them will fix the empty feelings inside. This attempt is what we might call the "quick fix." Looking outside yourself to solve problems rather than solving them first for yourself, makes you vulnerable to people who may try to take advantage of your feelings —and you may let them, or not even notice that this is happening. When someone comes along and offers themselves as the solution to your problems, he or she may overwhelm your otherwise good judgment about people, and the result is that without thinking you jump into a relationship before you are able to see if there are things that are hidden from view that in the future might cause you problems and in the end be hurtful to the long-term relationship you are seeking.

Here's the important, but sometimes difficult, fact. Once you feel more secure, better about yourself, more independent and even happy just to be who you are and where you are without needing to be in a relationship with someone, then you are ready to begin, but before you do, think first about what kind of relationship you are after and the kind of person you may be looking for. Some people want "flash and excitement." Other people simply want good companionship and something less exciting but perhaps more reassuring or enduring in the end.

When you find someone you are interested in, then the next phase of your work begins. Again, don't rush into anything. Take your time and evaluate this person from many different angles. Observe that individual in various situations so you can begin to get a more complete picture about who he or she actually is. You want to find out more about this individual's personal habits and past relationships. You want to know their complete history not just what they may be telling or showing you now. You want to know if they have the ability to make long-term commitments, or are have they just been moving from one relationship to another. What have their past relationship been like? Have these relationships been stable? If there was failure in a past relationship, has this individual been able to evaluate that failure, take some responsibility for it, and move on? Or do you hear from this individual that these failures were not their fault at all, and others were to blame—explaining away any personal responsibility for what happened? "The best predictor of future behavior is past behavior"

Ed Wagoner

Then you want to observe and see whether or not some of the following things are evident in this individual. Is this person, for example, willing to communicate their feelings, and talk about their issues openly with you without being defensive or blaming you? How flexible is this person on issues of importance to you, or to them? Do they show flexibility, and willingness to think about your needs and feelings as much as they do theirs? Are they able to discuss options to various issues or concerns that might arise in your relationship? Do they look with you for "win/win" solutions for both of you, rather than solutions that only benefit them? All of these are things you want to know about before you establish any long-term relationships.

Whatever failures I have known,
Whatever errors I have committed,
Whatever follies I have witnessed in private
and public life,
have been the consequence of action without
thought.
Bernard M. Baruch

You have to count on living every single day
in a way you believe will make you feel good
about your life,
so that if it were over tomorrow,
you'd be content with yourself.
Jane Seymour

Searching For The Light

He has achieved success who has lived well,
laughed often and loved much;
who has enjoyed the trust and love of good
people;
Unknown Author

Ed Wagoner

Chapter XV

Sexual Behavior

As a human being, it is one of our strongest (drives) priorities in life to have relationships that include sex. As a socially responsible human it has to be one of our priorities and values in life to have healthy responsible sex, which is sexual behavior that is consensual, guilt free, and causes no problems for our partners or ourselves. Our goal, therefore, needs to be to meet our sexual needs in a fully responsible manner. Sex activity becomes harmful when it is used to meet our needs at the expense of others, or is used as a form of entertainment, or to influence, manipulate or control others. Sexuality can be used to obtain resources, money, attention, or benefits, which causes the object of our sexual behavior, or ourselves, to be hurt or harmed physically or emotionally. Sex is also harmful to others and us when it is practiced in a manner that is illegal as defined by the penal code or violates the rules and codes of society. These laws and rules are usually very similar and designed to prevent harmful or anti social behavior. We may not always agree with these laws and social rules but we must understand that the reasoning behind them is the greater good for all.

Meeting our sexual needs is one of the greatest paradoxes we face in our lives. We have both physical and psychological drives that push us to meet our sexual needs and to enjoy sexual behavior. We also, at the same time, have a host of sometimes contradictory information, social values, rules, and laws that make getting our sexual needs met more complicated.

We have to understand the complex forces surrounding sexual behavior to fully appreciate the difficulty we face in our efforts to have healthy sex. There are both biological and psychological forces that affect our ability to make wise decisions concerning who and when we should become sexually involved with someone. It is commonly believed that we have primal forces within each of us that drive us to pleasure or immediate gratification. (The Libido was one of Freud's theories). We know that we have pleasure centers in the brain that release biochemical's to reinforce our pleasure and motivate us to seek immediate gratification. Our ability to use rational and logical thinking and our knowledge of potential consequences keep these forces in balance and sometimes in check. That is, if we are fully aware and informed of the potential consequences and we choose to take the time to think about consequences and negative outcomes. To our misfortune we also have the ability to not use this more rational part of our brain and go blindly headfirst into the pleasure and immediate gratification. These internal forces are also impacted by our psychological state at the time we have to make critical decisions or choices as to what direction we go in. If we are in an emotional

Ed Wagoner

state, unhappy, sad, frustrated, angry, or alcohol or drugs impair our judgment, then it becomes more difficult to use our logical and rational parts of our brain to explore all of the potential consequences. We become more likely to choose something that brings us relief or diversion from our undesirable state. Pleasure and excitement become a lot more attractive in this regressed state. Regression is a process where we function at a lower level in our thinking and judgment and therefore our ability to make good choices is impaired. If we are unhappy with a relationship, job, health, life, or whatever situation we may find ourselves. The more vulnerable we are to making choices that bring us some escape from our discontent in an unhealthy way. This may push us to use alcohol, drugs, or some other form of distraction, which adds to our regression. We are also influenced by the media in our everyday life and choices we make as to forms of entertainment we may choose and the type of person we may want to have a relationship with.

It is true that in our society the Media uses sex (or the desire and attraction associated with it) to promote, sell, entertain and influence us on a daily basis. You might say we are pummeled with sexual stimuli. Our entertainment industry has now made it acceptable to have multiple sexual partners with little if any commitment, suggesting we can change them as frequently as we want with no obvious consequences. The moral and value codes portrayed by the media are becoming looser with each new season. Our families and children are now able to watch soft porn on television. Hard core pornography is readily available on the Internet, and almost any site you rent movies. This is all part of our immediate gratification or pleasure oriented side and because it is on TV we and our children get the message that it's appropriate for us to watch it and enjoy it. The values we are hopefully taught by our family and Religion tell us to be more responsible. But our subconscious drive (Libido according to Freud) encourages us to seek pleasure. We have to develop our conscience, values and morals and internalize them (make them a part of our everyday decision making) to keep from falling into the immediate gratification, pleasure seeking trap.

So what is the problem with pornography? After all it is legal. And what is wrong with a little sexual action in our movies and on television and books? After all it's exciting to watch. The first problem is it is acting, not usually true to real-life circumstances. Its acting, fantasy, produced to get your attention and your money. Unfortunately some people begin to see this sexual behavior as desirable, the way it could be, the way we want it to be. This leads to a distorted sense of reality and when it doesn't happen for us in our world we feel something is wrong and we become unhappy with our partners or angry because our partners don't act like the people on the movies or shows we watch. We are thinking with our pleasure-oriented part of our brain and can become focused on

Ed Wagoner

trying to find this type of sexual behavior to engage in. This can lead to unhealthy thinking and behavior such as infidelity, prostitution, or in the worst case things like rape, child sexual abuse, and a variety of other deviant or socially unacceptable sexual behaviors. Secondly we get use to more socially questionable, maybe borderline deviant sexual behavior. This can make us less satisfied with "normal" sexual behavior. At best it can lead to the breakup of an otherwise healthy relationship.

To further complicate matters we are discouraged or afraid to talk with our significant others or anyone else about our thoughts and feelings about sex. Many people feel they have to be proactive about sex and act like the people in the movies and on television. They want their wives, husbands, and significant others to cooperate with their fantasies (or the visual images in the media) to meet their sexual desires. They think this is what their friends expect of them and fear being criticized to act any other way. Some people have been given the impression that sex is dirty and they should not enjoy it or engage in forms of sexual behavior that do not lead to pregnancy. This makes it difficult for them to enjoy sex, especially if it pushes the boundaries of what they believe is normal. Many of us do not receive any realistic or helpful information on sexuality and healthy sexual behavior as we are growing up. As a result we learn all sorts of inaccurate, unhealthy, and often inappropriate ideas about sexuality. Frequently we learn how to meet our sexual needs by trial and error. This leads to bad experiences and guilt that can further complicate our efforts to get our sexual needs met in a healthy responsible way.

Unless we have parents or someone else we listen to give us accurate and helpful information and teach by modeling healthy relationships. Things like self respect, open communication about boundaries and personal rights to choose, and then we have to learn on our own how to deal with sexuality.

The good news is sex can be great and guilt and consequence free if we develop and practice a few basic rules and values. We must be committed to an assertive style of sexual behavior. We will require that our significant others treat us with respect and the choice to engage in sexual behavior is only made in a mature, responsible and well thought out manner weighing all potential consequences and problems carefully. We will only get involved in a mutually respectful relationship meaning we will give our partner the same respect and ability to make well thought out and responsible decisions. We must never take advantage of persons who are not able to think clearly and make informed choice to consent. It is not appropriate to be sexual with persons who are impaired in any way, in any emotional state, immature, needy or simply too young to properly consent. If we cross this line it can lead to criminal consequences. Everyone needs to understand this reality. We must be honest about our intentions and degree of commitment. We need to make every effort to not harm our partners physically or emotionally and fully understand their ability to consent..

Our goal should be to enter into a mutually committed relationship with a person who cares as much for us as we do for them. The relationship will be based on honesty, respect, and consideration for each other's goals and boundaries. Healthy sex will be a part of this relationship as well as healthy intimacy. Ideally we will communicate freely with another about our feelings, fears, wishes and desires, and our feelings will be listened to and treated with respect. This should open doors to build a guilt and remorse free relationship that enjoys healthy sexual activity.

Chapter XVI

Becoming a Wise Person

Wisdom is a gift. But strangely it is not a gift that we simply receive from others. More importantly, it is a gift we can actually give ourselves. This raises two questions: what is wisdom and how can we give ourselves its gift?

One of the goals in our work is to grow up and become mature, well adjusted, socially responsible human beings. This is one of the definitions of wisdom and is a goal that every human being should aspire to, and most human beings accomplish it. Our ultimate goal is to reach balance and maturity in such a way that we can apply it wisely to all the activities and decisions we make throughout life.

It is important to realize, however, that achieving wisdom and maturity is not limited to someone with a high IQ, or to someone who has special talents or associations that give them power and standing in society. Wisdom is available to everyone and can be gained by anyone no matter who they are. Wisdom is a basic, fundamental insight into the way the world works and how to live in it successfully that comes from slowly (step by step) making the right choices. Wisdom is not gained quickly; it comes over time as we learn what is really important and what is not. Many people believe that success is in possessing material wealth, or having things like power or status, but a wise person knows that it is far more than having these things. A wise person uses his or her value system not simply to choose things, but to choose friends, associates, and what actions to take in life that will lead to a peaceful and well-balanced life.

If a person endeavors to make the right choices, then that individual is set upon a path toward wisdom. Inevitably, however, mistakes will be made. Everyone makes mistakes. A wise person is not someone who makes no mistakes, but someone who learns from his or her mistakes. Also a wise person is someone who can learn from other people's mistakes. We see examples of wisdom and folly all around us. We get to watch people as they choose wisely or unwisely and then we can observe what the outcomes actually are. A wise person studies these things, and watches carefully how life unfolds and what the positive and negative result of making certain choices are. Although we inevitably will make mistakes, we can avoid mistakes by simply watching what happens around us and learning from it all. A wise person is not someone with a high IQ, but someone who sees what others do and incorporates those lessons into his or her life.

You have certainly heard about people who are "street smart." But the question is, are they wise? The difference between them comes in whether or not an individual is making ethically moral decisions or whether he or she is simply making decisions that are self-serving (that get them what they want in terms of immediate gratification), but in the end are not wise. No matter how "street smart" you are, if your decisions are based on greed, dishonesty, lying, or are ego-centric or self-serving they will lead to negative consequences. Clearly that is not wise and will keep you from gaining wisdom. Now a wise person may make a decision that turns out to be self-serving and unwise, but when the negative consequences show up, that person learns from it and does not allow it to happen again. This is the kind of learning we are talking about, and the kind of wisdom that a maturing person eventually gains through all the experiences of life. In the end, that person will possess one of life's greatest treasures, the gift of wisdom.

> If you keep on doing what
> You have always done.
> You will keep on getting
> What you've always got.
> Unknown Author

> Wise men learn more from fools
> than fools learn from wise men.
> *Cato*

> A fool tells what he will do;
> a boaster tells what he has done;

Ed Wagoner

a wise man does it and says nothing.
Unknown Author

The wise learn from tragedy;
the foolish merely repeat it.
Michael Novak

From the errors of others
a wise man corrects his own.
Publius Syrus

Wisdom is knowing less
but understanding more.
Unknown Author

When a man lacks wisdom his mind is always restless, and his senses are wild horses dragging the driver first here and then there. But when he is full of wisdom his mind is collected and his senses become tamed horses, obedient to the driver's will.
Unknown

Chapter XVII

Core Values and Basic Beliefs

Values Clarification

Every human being acts on what he or she feels to be his or her own basic values or beliefs that are the core of one's life. We do things because we think they are right, or because we ought to do them, or because we have some feel inside that we must do them. That feeling and foundation for our action is the core of our personal values. We each have these core values whether or not we know exactly what they are or can express them in words. As we grow and change, it is very important that we come to understand what they are, and if we discover that they are weak or need changing in some way, then we must do so with a good understanding of what they are and what we are going to do about them. So let's explore this inner foundation of our actions and behavior—our personal, core values.

We grow up in families and communities where we learn to think and act like the people around us. We are shaped by the values and beliefs of the people and families that we live with. We also learn these beliefs in school, in church, and in the associations we have with others in our day to day world. It is also true that we sometimes mimic the values and beliefs of others without actually accepting them for ourselves. Sometimes we do that because it is to our advantage, and because it will help us get what we want in life or benefit us at the time. At other times we simply repeat what we have seen and heard because we do not know of anything else, or what else to do.

Here are some core values which are common and basic to society that most of us hold. These seem to be absolutely necessary if we are going to live in a society which works for everyone, and which provides safety and security for all of us and help us get along with one another:

- The basic rule is: "Do unto others what you have them do unto you." This is called the "golden rule" and is universal around the world.
- Being honest and fair in dealing with others in the hopes that others will treat us fairly as well.
- Treat people with respect.
- Do not steal, lie to, or cheat them.
- Don't take advantage of others.
- Be considerate of others.
- Show empathy or care for other people.
- Take responsibility for whatever mistakes you make.
- Apologize when necessary.

These are basic and important for all of us. They exist around the world as universal principles that every culture, religion and civilization follows. There are, however, other sets of core beliefs and values that we hold which help us grow, or realize our full potential. If we live them, they improve and strengthen our lives. We could outline these in this way:

- The value of achieving things in life by having a good "work ethic." It takes hard work to accomplish things and hard work is ultimately good for us.
- All things worth having take time and effort to achieve, and we must have the desire and motivation to put time and effort into what we want in life.
- No one else can give you what you want. You need to take responsibility and work it out for yourself.
- Whatever we seek to accomplish for our own satisfaction or pleasure, however, should never be at the expense of others.
- My own sense of self worth does not come from what I have (or own), but from what I have been able to achieve through my own efforts.
- A good sense of myself comes from having done what is right by others and for myself, and this gives me inner peace.
- If I am at peace, then I find healthy and positive ways to enjoy myself which not only bring me enjoyment, but enrich my life as well as the lives of others.

As we consider these core beliefs and values, and as we live and act upon them, it becomes clear that they have power in our lives. When they come from within rather than being imposed by someone or something on the outside of ourselves, then they are even more powerful. This is what is often called internal control because it means we are in-charge of our own life and how it turns out and someone or something else is not in charge—like the Law (legal system), for example. The opposite (the Law) is called external control and means that we learn to do things (or not do things) because of their potential effect on us, but not because we really think they are right for us. We do them, instead, to avoid negative consequences—getting into legal trouble, for example.

When we live by internalized values, we decide what is important, and that takes priority over other factors (like peer pressure) that could move us into a negative direction. So each of us lives between two extremes, it seems. On the one side are the demands that we feel for "immediate gratification" (getting what we want when we want it, which is usually "right now!"), and on the other side, the potential negative consequences of some action that we might actually want to do, but we know that if we did them we would get in trouble. We exist between these two points of power in our lives. But if we have a core set of values, then we will be able to find our own way, and make our own path, without either of these two ends of the spectrum being the total motivating factor in deciding the way we are going to behave and what we are going to do.

There is also another set of forces that is actually better for us than the one described above. In this range we live between what makes us feel good about ourselves and our own peace of mind to live (and grow stronger as a result), on one side, and the desire and ability to accomplish good things and building better relationships, on the other. We live in the middle between these. If we think well of ourselves, making the right choices by using both sides of this scale creates a positive feeling inside of us. We are rewarded because we have a good feeling about ourselves and a sense of being healthy on the inside. Also, we are rewarded because others show us more respect, and want to associate with us more. We are rewarded as well because of the support which grows up around us and helps us becomes stronger and better just because people are beginning to trust our good qualities.

Core Values

Your Core Values are your inner truth, the things out of which you yourself are made. They are the things you truly believe in though you may never have put words to them. They are what make you, you. They are what you do when you're not even thinking about it. You may have ideas, opinions and beliefs that are part of your society, culture, family, or upbringing. You may "believe" in these things as ideas, but they are external in some ways to the real you. The way you live, without such thinking, however, are your core values. Your values can grow, and some, perhaps, can change, but that change should always be for the better, in the direction of growth.

Definitions for Core Values

Acceptance: the ability to be receptive to and work with life as it comes to you as something that is manageable, trying not to over-control the circumstances of life, but seeing them as opportunities for learning and personal growth. Acceptance looks at life as an opportunity to learn and not simply a challenge to be overcome. It means that we receive life as a kind of gift from which we can receive much if we give it our best. Acceptance does not resist life and its lessons, but is open to them and to what one can learn from others and from one's own experience, not matter how difficult.

Adaptability: when life presents us with circumstances that are unexpected (surprising or even painful) to be able to be flexible and adjust or refocus to these new circumstances as quickly and as easily as possible.

Balance: life is often a series of swiftly changing events and circumstances. It is easy to become unstable. Balance is steadiness, stability and adaptability in the midst of change. Keeping one's feet and learning to move with the flow of time and circumstances. Balance is a product of flexibility. It is staying in the "middle ground" and avoiding extremes which put a person in a position of inflexibility. Find the "middle way"—the path that threads through the extremes allows a person to stay balanced.

Bravery: does not mean one is never afraid, but to have courage in the face of inner fear and outer difficulty, and learning to meet the challenges without turning back or running away honestly and with a sense of purpose and care. Bravery is a balance between cowardice-fear and aggression-anger. The ability and courage to do what is right. Someone who is assertive and strong in making the right choices and being sure that those choices are also fair for everyone. A willingness to be strong and fight for what is right but not through aggression, but by being direct and assertive.

Compassion: is an ability to show concern and care for others as one would for oneself. It means to be aware of the needs and feelings of others and being willing to help meet those needs as one is able. Compassion comes from empathy, the ability to understand another person and know how the actions you take and the way you speak affects other people. It is the ability to cage how certain actions will hurt another individual and what would be fair to that individual. Compassion is also the opposite of ego-centrism and narcissism.

Contentment: is a sense of satisfaction and peace with life. It is also a sense of pleasure and well-being in a world where things change or one may not have everything that one wishes for. It means not always comparing oneself to others, but being happy with what one already has without trying always to acquire more. Contentment, however, is not necessarily the same thing as happiness which is often associated with the constant search for personal pleasure and meeting one's needs through immediate gratification.

Discipline: is the ability to have strength, commitment and focus in the face of life's difficulties. It also means to stay focused and to move forward even in the face of something hard or difficult. Not to give up easily and to show restraint when necessary, and to be able to think about the consequences of one's actions. The ability to pursue a goal without being easily distracted my immediate gratifiers in contrast to giving in to what is easy and fast and makes us feel good. Its opposite would be to avoid thinking of the consequences of our actions and, therefore, to get off track from our ultimate goals. Every accomplishment in life exercises discipline and focus.

Forgiveness: in life we experience painful events, some of which we did not cause or make happen, but which hurt us. Forgiveness is the willingness to remember the pain but pardon the pain-giver, not holding grudges and not trying to retaliate, but letting go and moving on. It is easy to get caught up in our feelings of anger, refusing to accept the role we may have played in a painful circumstance, and also refusing to accept that other people have faults just as we do. The ability to forgive is based on remembering these things and not blaming others for what they may have done, but accepting responsibility for the consequences of our actions and being forgiving.

Generosity: giving and receiving are part of the normal exchanges of life. Giving to others (being generous with your time and resources, being big-hearted and open-handed) in helping to meet the needs of others. This is something we can do willingly and graciously, or we can close our hands and seek only for ourselves. Generosity is the product of feeling secure enough, well adjusted enough to not be ego-centric. It allows an individual to focus on the needs of others and makes them willing to give out of their own resources to help others to make their own lives and circumstances better. This offering of oneself is also called altruism which is learning the value of others and the importance of sharing what you have with others. It is based upon a belief system that values a more selfless process of knowing that we are not the center of the universe but share it with others and there are willing to show hospitality by helping others with food and shelter, in a form of first-person generosity or altruism that gives directly person-to-person, and not just the 3rd-person generosity—which gives money to organizations and communities unrelated to oneself directly.

Gentleness: the world is full of harsh (cruel, unkind, unsympathetic) actions by people who only think about themselves. Gentleness means to act in a kind, tender or mild-mannered way so as not to intentionally harm anyone. It means to act with their feelings in mind and to treat them as you would want to be treated. At the heart of this value of gentleness is the basic attitude: **do no harm**. This is both an attitude toward the world around us as well as a demeanor, a way of being with the world and with others that says to others, "You do not need to fear me. I will not do anything intentionally to hurt you." This, however, does not mean that the individual who practices such a way of being with others is passive or cannot protect him or herself. When it is necessary the individual can protect not only him or herself, but also others, which understood as an act of bravery. But the individual projects a feeling that others pickup on which makes them comfortable being around this individual.

Good judgment: is the ability to make good decisions based on long-term goals and not meeting short term needs instantly and without fore-thought and consideration. Good judgment is a basic foundation for another value, wisdom. Good judgment is the result of being wise, which is also about the ability to think about the impact of the choices we make in a holistic manner—how are my choices going to affect not only me, but everyone else as well? Good judgment, therefore, is a lack of impulsiveness. It means we take enough time to make a good decision. We think through the consequences of our actions—how will what we do affect the lives of others around us, the lives of those we love? This value means that our decisions are judicious—that is, they use our education, our experience and the insights we have gleaned through experience to make a well thought-out choice. The result is we don't make pre-mature, quick decisions that hurt us and others in the end. (We don't make a "sales-pitch" for quick, immediate action to ourselves or to others that encourages us to act prematurely).

Honesty: the ability to speak the truth with frankness and candor without trying to change facts and hide intentions even if it means that the truth will bring pain or conclusions that

Ed Wagoner

temporarily put you in a bad light. This is perhaps the most fundamental and basic of the core values that we seek to practice. It is at the heart of the core-values because if you follow this value then most of the others will result as well. Honesty is, at its heart, not telling lies that hurt others and ourselves as a consequence. In the end, lies hurt us and others because they are deceptive and hide the truth. When we practice secrecy or dishonesty then what happens is more likely to be hurtful than helpful. We end up hurting ourselves and hurting others as a result. Honesty keeps you from hurting others. It gives another person the benefit of the doubt—"They know what I know. They see what I see because I'm not hiding anything from them." We often keep things secret out of fear that someone will take advantage of us, but this hides the truth and does not bring things into the light where everyone can act upon what is known.

Honesty must be balanced, of course, with being socially appropriate. Honesty does not mean that we blurt out everything we think, or our personal opinions. It may mean that we choose to watch and listen for awhile before we act or respond, or before we make "definitive statements" about something that we may need to retract later. So in dealing with others we need to learn how not to be deceitful with others, and yet not hurt others through our truthful statements about things.

This is, obviously, a balancing act. It is always a "work in progress." We learn both to be tactful and to be honesty. Again, our intention is to do no harm.

Humility: the ability to accept the way things are without exaggerating one's role or self-importance above others. It means staying modest and even unassuming when it would be an advantage to make demands for oneself. Humility is based on a good self-concept. One not only feels good about oneself, but also about one's environment without the need to put up a front or a façade of some kind or use power and position to get one's way. Humility means that one can act comfortably with other people without always bringing attention to oneself. It also means that an individual does not feel the need to impress others, or to impose one's own values upon others. Being humble means that each person is allowed to be who they are, and one is also willing to be oneself without pretension or affectation.

Integrity: when we are being authentically ourselves we are practicing integrity which combines honesty, truthfulness, honor and reliability together into the way we live and practice being in good relationship with others.Integrity is closely associated with honesty. It is the basic belief that who you are and what others believe about you are aligned. It also means that you are trustworthy because the outside (the way you present yourself and behave) matches the inside (the way you are and the way you think). The message that you send to others is that you are someone they can depend upon and trust because you are someone who will not take advantage of them. Your fundamental concept about yourself is to be a good person, and goodness is not simply what you do on the outside, but the way you are as a person deep-down. Integrity is also the way others come to value and respect you because there is congruence between the inside and the outside.

Kindness: means that we are able to show empathy, thoughtfulness and consideration for others in a practical way that will make a difference in their lives as well as our own. Kindness combines many of the qualities on this list. It includes generosity, gentleness, acceptance, and compassion. It is compatible with the capacity to be considerate of others as well as giving and sharing our own resources with others. It, therefore, expresses thoughtfulness for others.

Loyalty: we are being reliable and loyal to others and to our responsibilities and relationships with others when we are able to practice faithfulness and dependability, and be a trustworthy friend, spouse and companion to others. Loyalty is the ability to make commitments to others and the integrity to let someone know that we are "there" for them, not for the sake of something we can get out of the relationship, but because we care about them in a fundamental way. It also means that we would not do anything knowingly to make other people lose trust in us and to stay committed to another person even if we get into difficulty in the relationship. If difficulties should occur, then we will remain open, kind and honest with another person, and should a relationship need to end in some way that we will do so in a way that maintains integrity for both. We sometimes need to end relationship, and sometimes we need also to change commitments, but we do so in ways that do not harm others or fabricate excuses but trying to keep an honest and open working relationship even when the commitment is over.

Patience: when we are able to endure difficulties and have the staying power to be with painful circumstances with tolerance and lack of complaint, then we are practicing patience with ourselves and with others. Patience is a process of not over-reacting and thinking things through before taking action or making a decision. Patience is giving things time to develop and not getting anxious to push things along, but let them unfold in their own timing and way. It also means that we learn not to be irritated when things are not following our own agenda or in the timetable we imagined they might operate. People that we live with need their own opportunities to grow and learn without feeling undue pressure from us. It means letting them also make mistakes in the same way we have. To practice patience is an exercise in "control," meaning that we will put into practice "impulse control" and not act on the first thoughts that come to mind. We must learn to stay calm and not let emotions rule our decision-making process.

Perseverance: is the ability to be firm with your good decisions and resolve to stay with what you know is right even though it is difficult to do so because you have made it a determination that it is the thing to do.

Pragmatism: this is the quality of being level-headed and sensible when everyone wants to move to an extreme. It means staying with good common-sense and maintaining a kind of simplicity when people want to over-complicate things. Pragmatism and the use of good common sense is based on the ability to see the whole picture and not just a part of it, and so is able to choose the best and perhaps simplest route to getting things done. Having the larger picture is a form of insight that is able also to imagine consequences, what might happen given these circumstances, and not over-react, but staying calm, think about the best options that don't over-complicate a situation. A pragmatist is neither overly optimistic, nor is a pragmatist pessimistic. He or she stays balanced by seeing both the possibilities for something as well as planning for the problems—looking at all sides of an issue, and then understanding what can and should be done, and what role the individual should play in that outcome.

Responsibility: when we take responsibility for life we become accountable for all of it, and not just the part we like, staying dependable and conscientious even when it is not always to our advantage. Taking responsibility for things goes far beyond mere "self-care," and extends care to others. It means to be clear about what role one might have played in a situation, and how one may have contributed both negatively and positively to an outcome, and being responsible for that role. The opposite would be to be defensive, find fault with others to deflect blame, and not accept responsibility for our own actions—trying to make amends where possible. Taking responsibility means being able to think about consequences clearly and how our behavior, actions, and talk will affect others positively or negatively. When we do cause harm, it means also to be able to apologize for what we may have caused or done. Someone who is able to do this has a far better opportunity for maintaining stable relationships.

Ed Wagoner

Sincerity: is the quality of naturalness and genuineness where we stay true to ourselves, our values and our principles when the circumstances might dictate that we change them to gain an advantage. Sincerity is a stance toward life that says, what I say I will do and agree to do I take seriously. Others, therefore, can depend on me and my efforts to do what I agreed to because I am honest and keep the agreements and commitments I make to others. When someone is sincere, they mean what they say, and are not trying to take advantage of others just to gain benefit for themselves.

Trust (or Trusting): is the ability to stick with our convictions with a sense of confidence and hope that if we do not give up easily or without struggle that in the end what is good will prevail, and we will not only learn and grow but become better

Understanding: means that we are both able to know others and ourselves and to put both into a larger frame of reference that allows us to be thoughtful, considerate and observant and aware of what is really going on.
    Understanding involves the ability to put yourself in someone else's shoes and to see things, not just from your vantage-point, but from theirs as well. It involves empathy and caring for others, and also the ability to see

how one's choices and actions affect others and not just oneself.

Wisdom: is a kind of understanding, insight and good judgment that is gained not just from knowledge about things, but the experience of things through personal learning. The exercise of wisdom is the ability to apply to the immediate situation what one has learned in a practical and helpful way. Wisdom is an ultimate goal of all the work we do. It is the ability to understand thing in a comprehensive way—to see the bigger picture, and therefore to be able to think things through before making choices without over-reacting or being impulsive. Wisdom understands that it is often better to miss an opportunity now and try again later than to jump into something too quickly without adequate forethought or preparation. Wisdom represents stability, dependability, common sense, and good judgment all in one which allows us to use all the experience from which we have learned and to bring it to bear in a given situation. Wisdom is a constant learning. A wise person never stops learning and being willing to learn from everything—mistakes and successes, the negative as well as the positive events of life.

Each person has inside a basic decency and goodness. If he listens to it and acts on it,

Ed Wagoner

he is giving a great deal of what it is the world needs most. It is not complicated but it takes courage. It takes courage for a person to listen to his own goodness and act on it.
--*Pablo Casals (1876-1973)*

You are what you are
by what you believe.
Oprah Winfrey

Our fathers gave us many laws,
which they had learned from their fathers.
These laws were good. They told us to treat all people as they treated us; that we should never be the first to break a bargain'
that it was a disgrace to tell a lie;
that we should speak only the truth.
Chief Joseph

All the great things are simple,
and many can be expressed in a single word:
freedom; justice; honor; duty; mercy; hope.
Sir Winston Churchill

Chapter XVIII

SPIRITUALITY

Since the beginning of Human history man has attempted to explain the unknown forces of our world, We did not understand and feared the events of nature, storms, lightening, thunder wind storms, floods, droughts, earthquakes, volcanoes, tornados, hurricanes, fire, all sorts of what we now see as natural disaster. In addition humans, at least when they became capable of thinking and reason, began think about the concept of death and what become of us afterwards. This happened many thousands of years ago according to Archeologists. Humans capable of reasoning and communication needed to explain what was happening in the world around them. This was an ongoing process thousands of years before the written word and mans process of defining what religion was. The first groups of people who lived together in tribes or early civilizations explained these events by attributing them to powerful entities they typically called Gods. (Deity) There were usually multiple Gods, each having power over one or multiple forces man experienced. This has been suggested by philosophers as a necessary process for man to explain what goes on around him in the world and in life. In the last few thousand years the event of the written word has allowed man to communicate and define not only what his thoughts and beliefs are but combine the thinking of large groups of people and the wisest of those people. (Scholars) Note that only a few people had the ability to understand and document the written word in that era. Everyone else learned verbally through legend, folklore, and stories told in their families and community and by traveling scholars or storytellers. People, if allowed, developed their own beliefs based on the information they were provided in their families, community and what part of the world they lived in. Other people in the world were encouraged, (I will with caution use the word indoctrinated) to believe what they are taught without question. That leaves us today with over 40 major religions in the world. (The Big Religion Chart; Compare World Religions) Most religions believe in a higher power, one God and that God has the power over life and the afterlife. A few major religions believe in a different perception of what God is and what afterlife means. Atheists are considered a religion although they do not believe in a god or an afterlife. I think Charles Darwin brought up the concept for an intellectual argument about the existence of God in his book "Origin of Species" with the concept of evolution, he is attributed with having said " It is not the most intellectual or the strongest of the species that survives; but the species that survives is the one that is able to adapt and to adjust best to the changing environment in which it finds itself" He did not question religion and evolution does not say that Religion can't explain evolution. All religions are complete systems in that they can explain how and why everything happens. You just have to have faith. Albert Einstein was an agnostic, "religious nonbeliever," but he rejected a conflict between science and religion and held that cosmic religion was necessary for science.

Most Religions throughout the World believe their beliefs are the one truth and all other religions are inaccurate, a misconception or a corrupt interpretation of the Bible or written document they follow. It may be some version of the Bible, the Qur'an, the Torah, a different written or spoken interpretation of the Religion you believe. Many battles have been fought over what is believed to be an opposing, unknown, (We tend to fear the Unknown) and what is perceived as dangerous Religion or practice. The primary difference in Religions, I think is in beliefs, rituals, ceremonies, codes, and doctrines. All religions have basic core principles that are similar. These have to do with how we interact with and treat our fellow man. We may follow The Golden Rule, The Ten Commandments, The five or eight precepts (Buddhists), the five principles or ten disciplines (Hindus), The ten Yamas and Niyamas (Hindus) or Yin and Yang (Chinese) or just the idea of Karma. It simply breaks down to Mans Humanity or Inhumanity to Man.

Let's start with what I believe we do wrong. I'm going to use the seven deadly Sins as an example. "The Greek monastic theologian Evagris of Pontus first drew up a list of eight offenses and wicked human passions." In the late 6th century, Pope Gregory the Great reduced the list to seven items.

Pride: the lack of humility befitting a creature of God.
Greed: too great a desire for money or worldly goods.
Lust: impure and unworthy desire for something evil.
Anger: unworthy irritation and lack of self control.
Gluttony: the habit of eating or drinking too much.
Envy: jealousy of some other person's happiness.
Sloth: laziness that keeps us from doing our duty to God and man.

This is primary reason we need to understand and internalize a strong value system.

Empathy, humility, is a deterrent to pride. Honesty and appreciation of what you have are a deterrent to greed. Self esteem is a deterrent to sloth, gluttony, and over indulgence. Patience and compassion are deterrents to wrath, anger and aggression. Gratitude is a deterrent to envy and lust. Spirituality is a deterrent to selfishness, unfairness, and egocentric thought and behavior. Our challenge in life is overcoming or managing our drive for pleasure, immediate gratification and desire. We have to learn to manage our needs.

Searching For The Light

Our needs are innate, we are born with the physiological and neurological mechanisms to enjoy pleasure and have needs that we must meet to find that pleasure, happiness and peace. I think Abraham Maslow best explained our needs with his "Hierarchy of Needs". First we have to have the basic necessities of life, such as air, food, water and shelter from the elements. After these are met we can focus on companionship, attention, affection, tactile stimulation, intimacy, belongingness, relationships family, and friendship. Then we build on self esteem, recognition, respect, self control, competency, mastery, independency, and freedom. After we achieve these, and not everyone does, we can work on self-actualization, meeting our full potential, to accomplish all that one can. Maslow later added Self-Transcendence, giving one's self to a higher goal outside one's self. The concept of altruism, compassion and spirituality to the purpose of helping others meet their needs.

All religions core principles lead to this concept. It is described as seeing, finding the light. The word Apocalypse is a Greek word for lifting the veil. (Morgan Freeman in The story of God) The battle between good and evil is the effort to find the light. I was blind but now I see, (Christian bible.) Enlightenment is not about the end of the world as we know it. It is seeking the truth for here and now, no cataclysmic end, just an end to

Ed Wagoner

the self, self indulgence, self love, and self focus. (Ego centered behavior)

The purpose of life is to end suffering. We suffer because we continually strive after, desire, things that do not give us lasting happiness. Life is a journey. Death is the return to earth. We must strive to attain enlightenment. (Buddhist philosophy)

Spirituality is necessary to find peace in life. Whether you believe in a God or not you should be a spiritual person. If you become an altruistic, compassionate, and spiritual person, do no intentional harm, accept responsibility for your life and deeds, strive to help those less fortunate, then you will receive whatever benefits this life and the afterlife have to offer. **You will have found your Light.**

"The belief that there is only one truth, and that oneself is in possession of it, is the root of all evil in the world."
Max Born

Friedrich Nietzsche saw the process of becoming oneself is governed by the willingness to own one's choices and their consequences-A difficult willingness, yet one that promises the antidote to existential hopelessness, complacency, and anguish.

"Religion is to do right. It is to love it is to serve, it is to think, it is to be humble."
Ralph Waldo Emerson

"We go into religion in order to feel warmer in our hearts, More connected to others, More connected to something greater and have a sense of peace."
Goldie Hawn, Beliefnet interview

"Relation of human beings to God or the Gods or whatever they consider sacred or, in some cases, merely supernatural."
Britannica Concise Encyclopedia (online, 2006)

"Religion consists in a set of things which the average man thinks he believes and wishes he was certain of."
Mark Twain, Mark Twain's Notebook (1879)

"Man is the Religious Animal. He is the only Religious Animal. He is the only animal that has the True Religion-several of them. He is the only animal that loves his neighbor as himself, and cuts his throat if his theology isn't straight. He has made a graveyard of the globe in trying his honest best to smooth his brother's path to Happiness and heaven."
Mark Twain "The Lowest Animal"

"Religion is an illusion and it derives its strength from the fact that it falls in with our instinctual desires."
Sigmund Freud, New Introductory Lectures on Psychoanalysis

BIBLIOGRAPHY

www.pravmir.com/the-seven-deadly-sins-introduction/
Sigmund Freud, The Ego And The Id,1923b
Sigmund Freud, Repression,1915d
Sigmund Freud, The Psychopathology Of Every Day Life, 1901b
Sigmund Freud, An Autobiographical Study, 1925d
B.F. Skinner, The Behavior of Organisms: An Experimental Analysis, New York, Appleton-Century. 1938
B.F. Skinner, Science and Human Behavior. Macmillan. 1953
Diagnostic and Statistical Manual-5, 2013 American Psychiatric Association
En.wikipedia.org.wiki>Normal_distribution 2024
https://www.braineyquote.com>authors>albert-einstein
https://en.wikipedia.org>wiki>Albert_Einstein
https://en.wikipedia.org/wiki/Religions_and_philosophical_views_of_Albert Einstein
Hare, R. D. (2003). Manual for the Revised Psychopathy Checklist (2nd ed.). Toronto, ON, Canada: Multi-Health Systems.
http//en.wikipedia.org/wiki/Jean_Piaget
https://www.brainpickings.org/2018/12/19/hiking-with-nietzsche-john-kaag-eternal-return/
https://religionfacts.com/religion
https://linkedin.com/pulse/reach-your-potential-through-self-actualization-advice-cory-galbraith
http//en.wikipedia.org/wiki/Abraham_Maslow

http//en.wikipedia.org/wiki/Charles_Darwin/ " on the Origin of Species"
https://medium.com?the-mission/25-things-you-should-give-up-if-you-want-to-be-happy-790f9eece5d4
https://www.psychologytoday.com/us/blog/beyond-school-walls/202305/10-core-values-to-guide-behavior#:
Schiraldi, Glenn R. 2001.The Self-Esteem Workbook. New Harbinger Publications
Schiraldi, Glenn R. 1999. Building Self Esteem. Chevron Publishing Company.
McKay, Matthew & Rogers, Peter, 2000, The Anger Control Workbook. New Harbinger Publications
W. Doyle Gentry, Ph.D 2007. Anger Management for Dummies. Hoboken, NJ: Willey Publishing, Inc.
En.m.wikipedia.org. Anger Management 2024.
Burton, J. (1990) Conflict: Resolution and Prevention. New York: St Martin's Press
En.m.wikipedia.org. Conflict Resolution 2024
Smith, Manuel, 1975, When I Say No, I Feel Guilty. New York: Bantam Books
Alberti, Robert E. & Emmons, Michael, Your Perfect Right: A Guide To Assertive Behavior. San Luis Obispo: Impact Publishers, 1977
En.m.wikipedia.org. Assertiveness 2024
Big Religion Chart: Compare World Religions, religionfacts.com 2004-2024
Branden, Nathaniel, The Six Pillars of Self-Esteem, Bantam, 1995

Ed Wagoner

https://www.mayoclinic.org/healthy-lifestyle/adult-health/in-depth/self-esteem/art-20047976?p=1
https://awarenessact.com/7-ways-to-free-yourself-from-bad-karma/
https://www.theladders.com/carer-advice/the-10-qualities-of-an-emotionally-intelligent-person
https://www.linkedin.com/pulse/how-wisdom-can-change-your-life-deepak-chopra-md-official-?trk=eml-email_feed_ecosystem_digest_01-reccommend...
https://www.PsychSanDiego.org>downloads>CognitiveBehavioralTheoryCycle.
https://thoughtcatalog.com/liza-varvogli/2019/01/7-powerful-attitudes-you-must-have-in-order-to-achieve-any-change/
https://en.wikipedia.org>wiki>Stephen_Halking_Quotes
https://www.amanet.org>articles>the_five_steps_of_change
https://.en.wikipedia-ortg>wiki>core>values
Peck, Scott M. The Road Less Traveled: A New Psychology of Love, Traditional Values
Spiritual Growth (Simon & Schuster, 1978)
Whittle, Lisa>whole_honest_look_holes_life_amazon_2011
www.lifehack.org/889057/books-on-relationships
wwwe.lifehack.org/home>life potential>What are the Core Values? 31 Core Values to Live By
https://religionfacts.com/religion

www.ingramcontent.com/pod-product-compliance
Lightning Source LLC
Chambersburg PA
CBHW060322050426
42449CB00011B/2610